For distribution, contact and ordering information, please refer to the last page of this book.

© Copyright 2004 by Rev. J. W. Arnold
ISBN # 1-932667-11-3

All rights reserved. No part of this book may be reproduced in any form without written permission from Rev. J. W. Arnold.
The Pentecostals of Gainesville
8105 NW 23rd Avenue
Gainesville, FL 32606
(352) 376-6320
www.gainesvilleupc.net

Power Encounters

Transcribed from the audio / video series
preached by Rev. Jeff Arnold

A BookEnds Press Publication
PO Box 14513
Gainesville, FL 32604

POWER ENCOUNTERS

Chapter One   1
    When Jesus was risen

Chapter Two   33
    Ye men of Israel, hear these words

Chapter Three   57
    Unpracticed truth is no better than false doctrine

Chapter Four   77
    And when he came to his disciples, he saw a great multitude

Chapter Five   111
    Jesus was a man approved of God

CHAPTER ONE
When Jesus was risen

Mark 16: 9, "Now when Jesus was risen early the first day of the week, he appeared first to Mary Magdalene, out of whom he had cast seven devils. (10) And she went and told them that had been with him, as they mourned and wept. (11) And they, when they had heard he was alive, and had been seen of her, believed not." Now these are the people who had been casting out devils and healing the sick and cleansing the lepers. They had a hard time believing this lady.

Now there's a reason why I'm reading this: What you have accomplished in the past is no guarantee for your present situation. There has to be constant renewal in our levels of faith. These guys had done miracles, signs and wonders. These guys had been told by the mouth of Jesus, "I'm getting up in three days." When the lady sees Him and tells them, they're... "We don't believe that." Now that gives me encouragement. Guys like that...after being so involved in the miraculous could disbelieve a good report...there's hope for us.

(12) "After that he appeared in another form unto two of them, as they walked, and went into the country. (13) And they went and told it unto the residue: neither believed they them." Now this is the kind of stuff that Jesus has to work with to win the world. (14) "Afterward he appeared unto the eleven" ...and after getting advice from Jeff Arnold he fired all of those people.... "Afterward he appeared unto the eleven as they sat at meat, and upbraided them with their unbelief and hardness of heart, because they believed not them which had seen him after he was risen."

Unbelief and hardness of heart go together. What makes your heart hardened? Easy—tragedy, sorrow, adversity, setbacks, unfulfilled expectations, disappointments, unanswered questions, unanswered prayers. Lots of stuff can harden your heart. It doesn't mean you don't love God, it just makes your heart get hard, because God wants your heart soft and pliable and sensitive to the Spirit, and those things are the things of life that just harden it, so that when a good report comes you go, "Awe, Come on."

(15) "And he said unto them, go ye into all the world, and preach the gospel to every creature. (16) He that believeth and is baptized shall be saved; but he that believeth not shall be damned. (17) And these signs shall follow them that believe; In my name shall they cast out devils; they shall speak with new tongues; (18) They shall take up serpents; and if they drink any deadly thing, it shall not hurt them; they shall lay hands on the sick, and they shall recover. (19) So then after the Lord had spoken unto them, he was received up into heaven, and sat on the right hand of God. (20) And they went forth, and preached every where, the Lord working with them, and confirming the word with signs following."

Remember this thought: Two kingdoms in conflict—both spiritual and both powerful—and the Christian has been drafted into the army to battle. Therefore, we have to go forth, but we can't go forth unless we're clothed with power and authority in Jesus' name. I don't know about you, but this morning in my prayer session and again this afternoon, I was asking God if I was grieving Him, or if I am misunderstanding Him in that I desire to be equipped and clothed with power and authority? And I asked Him, "Am I supposed to feel anything or do I just talk?" Now I don't know how you feel about that, but it's nice to feel a little sizzle in your soul and a flame in your heart, and there's a quickening, and there's sometimes when you go to pray for people where you'll hit an unction of prayer and you'll feel an unction of God and the prayer just flows. But there are other times where it seems like it's arduous, and a task, and unenjoyable. You're putting time in and you're checking the clock.

John 10:10 says, "The thief cometh not, but for to steal, and to kill, and to destroy: I am come that they might have life, and that they might have it more abundantly." Now if you read into that, the truth you will see is that Jesus is saying, "At the present moment you neither have life, nor do you have it abundantly." They were alive, but they weren't alive spiritually. He says, "I've come that you may have life." Now life is not living. He's talking about a quality of life, a spiritual quality that would only come to people through the gift of the New Birth, which was going to happen at Pentecost.

Now here's what I want to talk to you about: understanding what our mission is. Our mission is simply to rescue souls who have been taken captive because of two things: Adam's fall and Satan's snares. Now if you look in 2 Timothy 2: 24, "And the servant of the Lord must not strive; but be gentle unto all men, apt to teach, patient, (25) In meekness instructing..." now watch the reason why it's not always easy to win souls here "...instructing those who oppose themselves;..." they don't even know that they're fighting against their own salvation. (25)...if God peradventure will give them repentance to the acknowledging of the truth; (26) And that they may recover themselves out of the snare of the devil, who are taken captive by him at his will."

You got two problems. You got people who are fighting themselves, and people who are snared, snatched, seduced by the evil one. So we have to get people first out of the snare of the devil, and sometimes you have to argue with people and debate people and pray for people and try to reach people to make them even realize that they're caught. Snare. What are snares? Snares are Satan's deceptions and seductions and his traps that are set by him to deceive people, to take people hostage and to hold on to them, so that he can keep them from becoming what God wants and God divinely intends, and in order to do that he must use his power.

My message is Power Encounters, and that's the issue. We need to understand that we are called to the Power Encounter. Jesus, according to Luke 4:16-18, He said that He has come to set the captives free. In fact, He says, "The Spirit of the Lord is upon me..." He's reading from the Prophet Esaias. He said that the Spirit of the Lord is upon me and has anointed me to preach the gospel to the poor and heal the brokenhearted. Now listen, that's as much a ministry as healing sick people in their physical infirmities. He said, "To heal the brokenhearted." We live in a generation that has more inner-healing needs than any other generation.

People suffer from fractured and ruptured relationships and problems and hatred and hurts and hemorrhaging in their hearts. People need a place where they can get inner healing. We're not offering psychosomatic stuff. We're not offering psychic healing. We're offering Spiritual healing that Jesus...has any one besides me ever had the Lord just heal you inside from a bitterness, or an anger, or a hurt, or a resentment, or a frustration? That's as real and as precious as having somebody walk, or see, or hear. That's just as real. He said, "I've come to heal the brokenhearted."

That's why psychiatrist's couches are doing a booming business. That's why counselors are working extra hours, because people have ruptured feelings, they're hurt inside and if that is not fixed...but...your life flows out of your inner man. Out of the heart flow the issues of life. There have been times that I have come to church that I have been physically well and I have been emotionally whacked. I can try to function, but you find that you function without unction. You function without a flow. Why? Because you're bleeding and hurting and you wish you could just pick up a phone and talk to someone. You wish you had somebody that was on the same wavelength as you. I'm not talking about Pentecostal crybaby stuff; I'm talking about just wishing I had a friend.

That's what happened with Elijah. Elijah ran into the wilderness and left his buddy behind and did the worst thing he could ever had done—he left behind his only source of encouragement. He was hurt and disillusioned and disappointed. He wasn't physically in trouble. He wasn't spiritually naked or destitute; he had power with God. But he had been emotionally traumatized by Jezebel's little note;

"I'm unimpressed with your nifty little tricks and don't know how you pulled it off. You made my ol' man look bad and you outran my chariots and I'm going to kill you tomorrow. Love Jez'."

And he was emotionally devastated, not because he was threatened, but because his expectation was that the miraculous and the supernatural would bring Jezebel to a place of repentance. Instead it hardened her. That's why when he went into the cave the Lord didn't chew him out. He didn't damn him and condemn him or ridicule him. He didn't just turn around and say, "What are you doing stupid?" He turned around and realized the guy was bleeding and hurting. So before he even got to the cave He sent an angel by and fed him twice and gave him some words of encouragement. He didn't turn around and say, "Why you stinkin' preacher, backslidden prophet, ain't got no courage? Why don't you just kill that old bag?" He didn't do any of that. He said, "Hey, you're tired, you're exhausted, here's some groceries. Here, eat and sleep and just lay down some."

You know, sometimes you can get more healed by just getting a good night's rest, instead of just staying all wired like a twelve-day clock. Just rest. Take a few rounds and just sit down. I feel like that preacher friend that says, "Oh, the world's lost!" Too bad God doesn't know it." Last time I checked He knew it! And you don't see God getting all wired up about it, saying, "Oh, what am I going to do? What am I going to do?" No, He's just going to work in a time frame and a season that He's given to us. Sometimes you just need God to say, "Come on, sit down, you're wired."

You know what happens? Your focus goes out. You read into things. You misconstrue things, a simple thing like a missed handshake or a look. ...Well, you just said hello to her and she was in between a hiccup and a sneeze and she couldn't say anything, and you read into that that she never did like you. That happens to us all the time.

I get notes every once in a while that people get offended, because I didn't shake their hand, or I forgot they're in the hospital and I didn't visit them. I get calls when I didn't visit people and they were in and out of the hospital in two days and didn't call the church and felt I should have known if I walk with God. I wanted to say, "I do walk with God and God told me to stay away from you, so you wouldn't ruin my day!" But I didn't, because I love you. Heal the brokenhearted.... Man, that'll give everybody in this church a ministry right now. To heal the brokenhearted. If you can't find somebody that's strained and struggling and hurting...man, you're deaf, dumb and blind. Man, people's countenance says a lot about their inner heart.

(18) "To preach deliverance to the captives, and recovering of sight to the blind, to set at liberty them that are bruised, (19) to preach the acceptable year of the Lord." Jesus came to set captives free. Acts 10:38, "How God anointed Jesus of Nazareth with the Holy Ghost and with power: who went about doing good, and healing all that were oppressed of the devil; for God was with him." Don't you wish God was with you? Jesus said, "don't think that I do the works, my father that dwells in me he does the works." So while I was praying this afternoon and this morning, it was almost like I answered my own prayer and I'm not God, I'm not called to answer prayer, but it was like I answered my own prayer while I quoted scripture to God. And I begin to tell Him about authority and power and I said;

"Well Lord, you said that it wasn't your flesh, it was the Holy anointing of God that was in you that made these things happen." And it was like...

"Right! And that's what's in you! And you keep wanting to *feel* something and I'm wanting you to *know* something."

What I'm trying to tell you is that Jesus Christ came to set captives free, and in order to accomplish His agenda, He would have to do it...here it is...through Power Encounters. And a power encounter is simply this: a clash of two opposite kingdoms. It's the very thing we don't want. Let's look at this; Luke 4:31, "And he came down to

Capernaum, a city of Galilee, and taught them on the sabbath days. (32) And they were astonished at his doctrine: for his word was with power. (33) And in the synagogue..." now watch this; what I'm trying to show you is He started His ministry with power encounters. His first one was at the beginning of Luke 4: the Bible says that Jesus, being full of the Holy Ghost, went into the wilderness and He confronted the devil. That was a power encounter. One kingdom against another. One ruler against another. A conflict, a clash, but guess what happens? This is so powerful...when there is a power encounter—coming out of that will be energy. It can come in a mess of an explosion; it can come in a mess of a flying-down-the-railroad-locomotive hitting a semi broadside. A power encounter sometimes gets messy. Whoever gets the most power wins. Everything else just gets scattered to the wind.

The Bible said when Jesus came out of the power encounter it released out of Him more power. Said He went in full of the Holy Ghost, but you find out when He comes back it says, "...and when he came out of the wilderness, he came out in the power of the Spirit." He went in full but, He came out in the power. What caused the release of the power? An encounter with an opposite force! Luke 4:14: "And Jesus returned in the power of the Spirit into Galilee: and there went out a fame of him through all the region around about." Why? Because the power, the energy that was resident in Him was released because of a conflict, because of combat, because of a collision, because of an impact with another force. Wait a minute...that force was inferior and Jesus ran over it!

You gotta get this; when you run over something, you know what? If you run over something and you run through something that's anti-God, not only do you defeat it, but you absorb into yourself whatever power it has. You take from it and you absorb it into yourself. That's why sometimes when you pray and you're in agony and you can't seem to push through, and then all of a sudden—*PUFF*—you break through a window or a doorway. You didn't just break through; the power disintegrated and you absorbed into yourself that which was against you. Watch this: said he (Luke 4:31) "taught them on the sabbath days (32) And they were astonished at his doctrine: for his word was with power." How can a person's word be with power more then voice and verbalization? There's got to be a demonstration to back up what's being said. (33) "And in the synagogue there was a man, which had a spirit of an unclean devil, and cried out with a loud voice, (34) Saying, Let us alone; what have we to do with thee, thou Jesus of Nazareth? art thou come to destroy us? I know thee who thou art; the Holy one of God." Watch...Jesus starts His ministry and He has a power encounter! The world that he's come to take and disassemble stands up in his face and he recognizes the authority and the power in Him and now he doesn't want to fight. You've gotta hear me. The same spiritual power that was in this demon possessed man was the power that fought with Jesus in the wilderness. When he was in the wilderness he said, "Let's rumble." When he came out of the wilderness he said, "I want nothing to do with you."

I'm trying to tell you, if we as a church can break through in just one realm of a power encounter, a lot of these pitiful little things that are tormenting us and driving us crazy, they're going to back away and say, "You can have your way." As long as you and I don't challenge it, as long as you and I don't confront it, then we play games in our minds. "...Well, I don't know if I'm big enough or powerful enough or great enough to knock it down...", but once you beat it...hhmm.

(35) "And Jesus rebuked him, saying, Hold thy peace, and come out of him." He didn't fuss and cuss and shake him and spit all over him for four hours. He said, "Shut your mouth and come out." And that devil that confronted Him said, "Yes sir!" Now watch this: He said, "Hold thy peace, and come out of him. And the devil had thrown him in the midst,..." See, he's going to get his last lick in. He threw him down. Watch; he's going to try to make Jesus look bad, he threw him down on the ground, "...And when the devil had thrown him in the midst, he came out of him, and hurt him not. (36) And they were all amazed, and spake among themselves saying, What a word is this! for with authority and power he commandeth the unclean spirits, and they come out. (37) And the fame went out into every place of the country round about."

Then he goes and he heals Simon Peter's mother-in-law of a fever. Then Verse 40: "Now when the sun was setting, all they that had any sick with divers diseases brought them unto him; and he laid his hands on every one of them, and healed them. (41) And devils also came out of many, crying out, and saying, Thou art Christ, the Son of God. And he rebuking them suffered them not to speak: for they knew that he was Christ."

Look at this: (42) "And when it was day, he departed and went into a desert place: and the people sought him, and came unto him, and stayed him, that he should not depart form them. (43) And he said unto them, I must preach the kingdom of God to other cities also: for therefore am I sent. (44) And he preached in the synagogues of Galilee."

I hope I'm making sense here, 'cause you gotta get this. Jesus' ministry was nothing but repetitive power encounters: Power of God, the power of devils, the power of diseases, the power of sin, the power of seduction and deception, deceit, evil, wickedness. Everywhere He went He had a power encounter. The problem is that you can't always govern the power encounter and make it be nice. Sometimes a power encounter gets messy. Watch this: Acts 2:22 "Ye men of Israel, hear these words; Jesus of Nazareth, a man approved of God among you by miracles and wonders and signs, which God did by him in the midst of you, as ye yourselves also know." Now, I use that over and over again about Jesus' credentials; miracles, signs and wonders. What are miracles, signs and wonders? Power encounters.

When I was praying...excuse me for being note-conscious, but I just got this before I came to service. In fact, I was 5 minutes late getting in here trying to write this down. When I was praying, I felt the Lord just quicken in me Ephesians 3:20. "Now unto him that is able to do exceeding abundantly above all that we ask or think, according to the power that worketh in us,...." And then the Lord took me to Zechariah and I saw in my mind Joshua, the high priest, standing before the Lord and Satan at his right hand to resist him, and the Holy Ghost said; "Power encounter, man trying to contact God; Satan trying to withstand him. Clash of power."

The poor man is caught in the middle. And I think He gave this to me to help some of you people who have problems with spiritual things. He said:

"Well, tell the people about natural medicine."

I said, "I've got lots of people that worship there."

He said, "Just tell them that in natural medicine, that's the clash between two powers; disease and remedy, sick and cure." He said, "When they take medicine, the medicine is a force and a power towards health, and it's gonna attack in their body what is making disease ravage there. Whichever one is more powerful wins." He said, "That's why, sometimes, if you take a medicine and it doesn't work, they may decide to give you a stronger medicine or an antibiotic. If you have an infection, or inflammation, and the antibiotic is a stronger power source, and it overcomes an infection, you end up with health." You see, we don't have a problem with it in the natural realm. This is what I got. Talk to Him tonight about the realm of education, for in the realm of education, it is nothing more then a power encounter.

Knowledge confronts ignorance. Truth challenges error. It's a clash. It's a clash! You're stepping into the clash with knowledge. You have the power of knowledge to help kids learn how to spell and add, talk and take care of themselves in life, and that power challenges ignorance and bad attitudes and upbringing and all kinds of stuff. But if the power is strong enough and the person is a receiver, the power of truth and knowledge overruns ignorance and you end up with a graduate. But all it is, is an encounter with power; whether it's mathematics, or spelling, or science, or physics, or geology, or biology, or whatever.

I was praying. This came to me. You know how my mind works...I get strange stuff in my head, and when I was praying this voice said, "How about construction?" Think of the power that is used to cut down a tree. Just pull the chainsaw when you are getting ready to cut it...the power of the chainsaw attacks the power of the fiber of the tree. Whichever is the greatest power wins, but in the midst of it there is all kinds of chips flying. There are all kinds of things cracking. In my mind I saw a great big building, and then all of a sudden there was a crane over here and out of that crane came this huge...what they call a medicine ball, and the thing just swung over and the power of that medicine ball hit the side of that building and knocked the whole building down. Crash...debris went everywhere. Dust and smoke and everything, and it said, "See, sometimes the power encounter is not neat."

And then it came to me again. He said, "What about boxing? What about wrestling? What about football?" Power encounters. "What about a bomb? What about an atomic bomb, a hydrogen bomb?" It's a power encounter. Parts clash inside, scientifically and chemically. Guess what happens? When they clash and they confront each other, there is an explosion and it expands and energy is released. How do we lift airplanes off the ground? How do we get rockets out of Cape Kennedy? There's a thrust that encounters gravity and whichever is stronger wins.

Jesus came out in the power of the Spirit. When you have a conflict and resistance, power and energy is always released. There's our problem. All the months that I taught on praise and worship, we still don't understand the power of praise and worship. Forces resisted.... Sometimes you don't want to throw your hands up. Sometimes you don't want to clap. Sometimes you don't want to say.... Forces are resisting. There's a power that's resisting that, because that power knows that if you or I break through in the realm of praise and worship, another power is going to be released that's going to dominate the power that has resisted us. Remember the story in the Bible it said that Moses...Michael contended with the devil about the body of Moses. See? Power encounter. The devil says, "I want the body", and Michael says, "You can't have it. I'm taking the body." And two powers, two governments, two kingdoms clash over a dead man's body.

The gospel is supposed to be declared and demonstrated in power. The Christian church has been called to clashes and conflicts with forces or systems that oppose…that resist Jesus' cause. That's why you have to have a gospel full of power. 1 Thessalonians 1:5, "For our gospel came not unto you in word only, but also in power, and in the Holy Ghost." Paul writes to the Corinthian church, 1Corinthians 2:1-5 that he came not with enticing words of men's' wisdom, but in power and demonstration of the Holy Ghost that your faith would not stand in the wisdom of men nor the words of men but in the power of God.

You've gotta hear me. Jesus was the embodiment of the power of the government of God. He was the embodiment of the Kingdom; He that came as God's invader into this planet. He says; I'm gonna upset everything that's here, I'm gonna clash with everything that's anti-God, I'm gonna take it apart, or I'm gonna disassemble it, I'm going to destroy it. …And then He leaves and puts you in charge and then you just go to church. And God's saying;

> "But you're the posse, you're supposed to get after the desperados, you're supposed to chase the villain, supposed to take the handcuffs off the hostages. Why do you just keep telling each other what you believe?"

Unbelief is the evil that we must confront and conquer. It is indeed the essence of Satan's kingdom—unbelief. So Jesus makes believers out of us through the gift of the Holy Ghost, and then appoints us as His royal instruments and vessels of His Kingdom. To do what? To confront evil, to expel it, to emancipate the victims, and to convict the lost. …It's just so fabulous?

Matthew 9:35, "And Jesus went about all the cities and villages, teaching in their synagogues, and preaching the gospel of the kingdom, and healing every sickness and every disease among the people."

Now I've taught you for months that preaching the gospel and healing the sick go hand in hand. Come on, the Lord Jesus Christ has made a double remedy for a double curse. 103 of Psalms: "Who healeth all thy diseases, who forgiveth all thine iniquities." Let me try it again; John 3:14, "And as Moses lifted up the serpent in the wilderness, even so must the Son of man be lifted up: (on the tree) (15) That whosoever believeth in him should not perish, but have eternal life." Now you understand, he's showing the fulfillment of the brazen serpent; but the brazen serpent took care of two things, and even the Pentecostal people don't say that. They only take care of one thing. Oh no! If you read the story of the brazen serpent, I think it's about Numbers 21, he turns around and says and the people came to Moses and said...we have sinned against God and we have spoken against you; therefore, pray to the Lord that we might be forgiven...and also he sent venomous and poisonous serpents among us and they bit us and we're dying.... So that's why they need help, for sin and they need help for disease. So he puts up a brazen serpent and everybody that looks, lives. So what did God do with them? He forgave their sins and He healed their sickness.

How would He do more for a brazen serpent then He would for a bleeding Jesus hanging on Calvary? He is also the healer of diseases and the forgiver of sins. God has provided a double cure for us.

Matthew 9:36-38, "But when he saw the multitudes, he was moved with compassion on them, because they fainted, and were scattered abroad, as sheep having no shepherd. (37)

Then saith he unto his disciples, The harvest truly is plenteous, but the labourers are few; (38) Pray ye therefore the Lord of the harvest, that he will send forth laborers into his harvest." Go to 10:1...now there are no divisions in the New Testament, they just did that in translations. There's really not Chapter 9, Chapter 10, Chapter 11...we just did it for translations, so it makes it easier to read, but he turns around in that last verse, Verse 38, "Pray ye therefore the Lord of the harvest, that he will send forth labourers into..." into what? "...into his harvest."

Now here's something I just got, I've never seen it in my life. Never seen it in my life. We always think He's saying pray for laborers to go out and win all these lost people. That's not what He's talking about. He's talking about the sick and the hurting. Go back to Verse 35 again. Watch: "And Jesus went off about all the cities and villages, teaching in their synagogues, and preaching the gospel of the kingdom, and healing every sickness and every disease among the people. (36) But when he saw the multitudes, he was moved with compassion on them...."

Now wait, watch what He's just done. He preached the gospel, He healed their sick, and He cast out devils, and He helped suffering humanity. Then He stepped back and He saw the lamentable condition that they were in and how they had to deal with hypocrisy and foolish religions that couldn't help them and His heart was moved with compassion and He turns around and He says that "the harvest truly is plenteous...." Wait a minute, what harvest? The harvest of suffering humanity! Whether the suffering is spiritual, emotional or physical, the harvest includes all suffering humanity. He looked at them and they were like sheep without a shepherd. They didn't have anybody to protect them, bind up their wounds, love them, heal them, and restore them. He was moved by it. And He said; ...oh the harvest.

I need to go back to Chapter 9:36-37 so everybody is talking the same way I am talking. When he saw the multitudes he's moved with compassion and then of course they fainted and they were scattered abroad as sheep having no shepherd. They had no direction for their life. They didn't have anybody to take care of them. Next verse; 37, then He says the harvest truly is plenteous. What harvest? That's what you were missing; at least I've missed it. What harvest? The sick, the hurting, the emotionally traumatized, the spiritually lost, the wandering, the listless: That's the harvest! He says they are plenteous, but the laborers are few. Verse 38, "Pray ye therefore the Lord of the harvest, that he will send forth laborers into his harvest. Chapter 10:1, And when he had called unto him his 12 disciples..."

I want you to get this: Jesus asked them to pray, and before they prayed He answered His own prayer; He said, (9:38) Pray ye therefore the Lord of the harvest, that he will send forth laborers into his harvest." In other words; "I ain't got time for you to pray. Here, here's the authority, here's power. Go into the harvest." Watch: He called the disciples, gave them power against unclean spirits to cast them out, to heal all manner of sickness and all manner of disease...no Holy Ghost, nobody's talked in tongues, Pentecost hasn't happened yet, and, yet, God has given them free Pentecost, authority to heal the sick, cast out devils. One writing says...raise the dead.

"But there hadn't been a resurrection yet!"

"It doesn't matter."

"I've got power and authority, I can give anything I want to give, raise the dead, heal the sick, cleanse the lepers...freely you receive, freely give. Listen boys and girls, you've received it freely, you didn't pray, you didn't get real spiritual, so I, somehow, had to give it to you. I, in my sovereign desire, gave you an ability, so you can help gather in the harvest. Now freely you've received. Now freely give it."

Folks, we're going to be indicted for not freely giving. There's only two reasons why we don't give: 1) We don't think we have it. 2) We don't care. Matthew 10:7-9, "And as you go, preach, saying, The kingdom of heaven is at hand." See? It's always the Kingdom. (8) "Heal the sick, cleanse the lepers, raise the dead, cast our devils: freely ye have received, freely give. (9) Provide neither gold, nor silver, nor brass in your purses." Now there's the kicker. There's something we've got a problem with. He said; ...I'm going to give you authority and power to do the job, but I want to keep you dependant.... I'm wondering if our independent American spirit hinders a flow of the miraculous.

He said; ...don't carry two shirts, two this...don't take an extra pair of shoes, and don't take this, and don't take that. Instead, I want you to be dependant.... Now me? I'd go with 3 MasterCard's, 2 American Express's, a Visa, a bag full of peanuts, Coke. He turns around and says; ...don't worry about groceries, just go to people's houses, and if the Son of peace is there your peace will rest on it, and if He's not there, bring it back, shake the dust off your shoes, let them stay sick...and oh, by the way, I want you to know the Kingdom of God came to your house, but you weren't worthy.... And He said; ...I'll take care of it later and I'm gonna tell that city and that household that it's going to be more tolerable for Sodom and Gomorrah than for you people, because I offered you the gospel of the Kingdom and you were so stupid and so self-centered and so religious you didn't want it. Folks, it ain't over when people reject. Don't ever believe it is. It ain't over when people don't want a Bible study and don't want to come to church and don't want the Holy Ghost. It ain't over! They've got Jesus on their hands now. Man, there's a bad day coming.

You've gotta please hear me; this is so powerful, so powerful. What is my subject tonight? Power Encounter. Two kingdoms clashing, forces, explosions, blood and guts, boom.... You say, "Well, I've never had a power encounter." Of course you have. Have you ever felt conviction? That's a power encounter. The power of another world encounters you and me and we're indicted because of our sin and shame, and we begin to cry and sob and weep. You've just encountered the power of God. Anybody in the house have the Holy Ghost? That was a power encounter. When the Holy Ghost fell and filled you with His Spirit, that was you encountering the power of another world.

Luke 10:16-19, "He that heareth you heareth me; and he that despiseth you despiseth me; and he that despiseth me despiseth him that sent me." Man, that's some power and authority for a believer. (17) "And the seventy returned again with joy, saying, Lord, even the devils are subject unto us through thy name. (18) And he said unto them, I beheld Satan as lightening fall from heaven..." don't be afraid of him. Every time you find him, he's falling down. (19) "Behold, I give unto you power to tread on serpents and scorpions..." wait a minute; let me help you with that. What does that mean? "I give you power to tread on serpents and scorpions." He's given you vindictiveness of what type of spirit it is; unclean, vial, sleazy, nasty, subtle, deceptive, killing. "I give you power to tread on serpents and scorpions." We're not talking about bugs. He's talking about spiritual powers.

Why do I need power? Because you need a power encounter to loose people of being held hostage, and they need a power encounter that's greater then the power that's holding them. They're being held against their will. They're being held hostage. They're being stolen away from God's Kingdom, so God says, "I want to get them back." You can't just walk in and say, "I rebuke you in Jesus' name." It ain't gonna happen. You'd better have some power. You better not be playing a game of the seven sons of Sceva... (Acts 19:13) "...we adjure thee by Jesus whom Paul preaches." Man, Hell jumped up and said, "Jesus we knew and Paul we knew but you're a faker, you ain't got no guts, 'cause you ain't got no goods, you're just a blowhard talkin' on somebody else's story."

That's why a lot of you don't pray for people who are sick. You leave it to me. You don't pray for the sick. Why? 'Cause it requires a power encounter. And you're taking your measurement by what you feel—"Well, I'm not worthy." Well, let's get that out of the way; you and I ain't never gonna be worthy. He's going to *count* us worthy. He's going to cover us with the blood and put us in the covenant and He's going to put an anointing on us...and now go ahead and pray...oohhh it got quiet now. Yeah? Wait 'til a few devils show up. You just walk up to that devil-possessed person and say;

"Hey! You get on out of there now and don't be ugly."

He's gonna say, "Who are you?"

"Oh, I go to the holly-roller church and Brother Arnold spits all over us and yells and screams at us all the time...and I'm going to defeat you with his sermon."

"I don't think so."

I don't want to hurt your feelings, but I have a feeling that a large percentage of you sitting here are scared of that. You are afraid of the devil. You are afraid of a confrontation. You're afraid of conflict. I'll prove it to you:

Last Wednesday, two young fellows walked in here with hoods on and hands in their pockets and I lost this service. You kept looking at them. "...I wonder if someone's going to shoot Brother Arnold....one of them is going to kill Brother Arnold, who's that boy?" You didn't know who it was, but it was two boys with hoods on and the whole temperature of this service changed, and I tried to focus but you kept going..."It might be a devil." I wish to God it was. See? Right now—tremendous unbelief. Listen pal, I don't have any authority over human spirits. I got biblical authority over devils. Say, "Well, I might get challenged." Jesus got challenged. The early church got challenged, but Jesus won and the early church won and this church is going to win if we don't back down, because we have been equipped by God to use the name of Jesus and the power of the Holy Ghost and the Word of God on everything that confronts us.

That's why we never go out of our way to talk to people with purple hair and rings in their nose and tattoos on their neck and the freaked-out and the whacked-out. Do you know why? "Might have a devil...." Wish they did. Right now I got you nervous, I can feel it. "...Hope none show up before this service is over." Well, I hope they do, I'm going to send them right to you. And then you're going to wish to God you hadn't watched all that video and TV. Don't you get it? Here's why we are afraid. We don't sense, we don't feel; therefore, we assume we ain't *got*. Wrong! The Book says that if you've got the Holy Ghost, you've got more power in you now then He gave those guys before Pentecost. You have "Christ in you, the hope of glory." So the sickness, or the devil, or the situation is not going to go away because you confront it, it's going to go away because the one that's inside you is confronting that situation as you release your faith and let that energy go. That's a *Power Encounter*. We all want to feel the power, but what do you do if you don't feel it? You've either got it or you don't got it. Come on, answer me, class. If you don't feel the power and you perceive the power, and Jesus said He'd never leave us nor forsake us, do you have the power?

So the only thing you've got to do is keep your flesh in submission and subjection. You can't play with sin. You can't be immoral in your mind. You can't be vial and trashy in your spirit and then expect the Holy Ghost to flow through you, because the vessel can hinder and restrict, just like it can cause flow. See...you think I'm crazy? Okay, you think I'm crazy. Let me show you in the Bible where God cast devils out of people with a piece of cloth. A piece of cloth! Now you talk about *me* being crazy—a piece of cloth. Now if we didn't have Bible for that you would have a right to say, "The man has lost his mind," but I've got scripture in the book of Acts that says God wrought special miracles from the body of Paul. Handkerchiefs and aprons were taken and they were sent to people. Watch. Two things happened: diseases departed, and evil spirits came out of them. Nobody prayed for them, nobody laid hands on them. God just did a special miracle. I'm here to tell you God can do special miracles in this auditorium. God can go outside what's written and do something that has never been done before. Yes he can!

There's a big difference between "unscriptural" and "nonscriptural." Anything that violates Bible is unscriptural. But there are things not in the Bible, they are nonscriptural and they will still be of God. There was no Bible precedent for what Paul did. And all the Bible thumpers could have said was, "My God in Heaven, man, the man's outside the Bible." "He's putting oil on hankies and picking up rags and sending them around the world." "The man has flipped out." Except when they wrote back and said, "All the devils went out of them folks and the polio left and the cancer left and the tuberculosis left and the AIDS left and everybody's getting healed...can we have another box of them hankies?"

Now wait a minute, you're not getting what I'm saying. You think I'm humorous. You know what that was? When that anointed handkerchief was sent out by the anointing of the Holy Ghost, it was a power encounter against disease and devils and the greater power won. Don't you get it? When we lay hands on you and we anoint you with oil and we pray for you, do you know what we are doing? We are looking for a power encounter. That's why, sometimes when we pray for you and the power gets to anointing you, you shake, you slobber, some people will fall down, some people will jump up and down. There's a power, there's an energy being released. It's an encounter.

That's why I've always hated this easy-believism:

"I believe in Jesus."

"Oh shut up!"

"I believe in Jesus."

"Really? You just met the Force, the Personality, the Creator and Sustainer of the whole universe and you were as blasé as a dead frog. I believe in Jesus? Man, you can't possibly meet the Creator of the world, have an encounter with God and you still fornicate and you still drink and you still steal and you still...oh, it can't happen my friend."

The encounter of God will create new desires in you. You may have shortcomings and failures in your life, but that desire will help you overcome them. You will become conformed. The image of Jesus Christ...we are in a process of holiness. We are in a journey trying to become more like Jesus.

Moses had an encounter with God. He had to put a rag on his face. Everybody I can find in the Book that had an encounter with God—they fell down on their face, they exceedingly quaked and trembled, shook terrified, the power of God was...and now we got a generation that..."Oh yes, I talk to Jesus all the time, in between "As the World Turns" and my fag show I'm watching. Yes, me and Jesus are praying...." Oh puke on you; I don't believe a word you are saying. Come on man, you've got to be kidding me. An encounter with God and then church is blasé? Life is mundane? You're not interested in clapping or praising and you say you've had an encounter with God?

How much mildew is on your encounter? Man, we need to get that junk off. You know the Bible says. "I shall be anointed with fresh oil." That's what I'm asking God to do in my life. I want to be anointed. I don't want to live in stagnation. I don't want to live my life by what I got from God ten years ago or ten weeks ago. I need fresh manna. I need fresh oil. I need a fresh sense of his presence. I can't live by memory. And I'll tell you something else; you can't live by inspiration, either. Inspiration is the worst octane to run your life on.

Knowledge. Power. Power Encounter. Here it is: "They'd been with Jesus." They didn't believe a word they were saying about their gospel, couldn't do anything about that lame man that was standing up looking real good, hadn't walked for over...couldn't say anything about a notable miracle: and they took notice. They had been with Jesus. Well, how do you know? Well, the encounter will come out in an expression. There will be a demonstration and a declaration

Mark 1: 14 "Now after that John was put into prison, Jesus came into Galilee, preaching the gospel of the kingdom of God, (15) And saying, the time is fulfilled, and the kingdom of God is at hand: repent ye, and believe the gospel." Then He goes and gets a hold of Peter and the boys and tells them to leave their fishing nets and come and follow Him. Verse 22, He comes down, "And they were astonished at His doctrine: for he taught them as one that had authority, and not as the scribes." (23) And there was in their synagogue a man with an unclean spirit; and he cried out, (24) Saying, Let us alone..." that's how you can always tell what kind of spirit you have. Any kind of spirit that wants the preacher to leave him alone is not of God. "Leave me alone!" That's a devil's spirit. "Leave me alone." "Don't tell me how to look or to live." "Don't tell me what to do." "Don't tell me about praying." "Don't challenge anything in my life." That's a devil's spirit!! You don't ever want God to leave you alone. You'll end up like King Saul, "God doesn't answer me by dreams." "He doesn't talk to me by the prophets." That's the most tragic thing you or I could have in our lives is for God to stop talking to us. I'd rather have God chastise me every day, slap me around and make me feel bad and put me on my face. Don't leave me alone! I'm not smart enough to get to Heaven.

Verse 25, He turns around and rebukes the devil and tells him to come out. He came out in Verse 26. What new doctrine is this?—Verse 27...when with authority he commands even unclean spirits and they obey him. Then he goes down to Verse 30 and heals Simon Peter's mom like the other one and then she lifts up and takes care of everybody. Verse 32, and even when sun did set they brought unto him the diseased and possessed with devils. All the city was gathered at the door and he healed many of sick divers diseases and cast out many devils and told the devils not to speak. He goes down in Verse 38 and says; ...Come on, I gotta go to the next town and preach" He said; I come forth to preach there, and he preached there in the synagogue, and he cast out devils and the next verse says and he healed the leper. And He just heals everybody.

Don't you get what He's doing? Everywhere Jesus is going is a power encounter. He's contacting and conflicting with the power of evil, whether it shows up as emotion, or physical infirmity, or spiritual negating. He's contacting them and confronting them. There's going to be an explosion. I hate to tell you this folks, but there are not any gentle, clean-cut conversions. The curse of Christianity today is they have this clean-cut conversion stuff. Man, you can't get stuff out of you with out an upheaval. Man, there's stuff in me still, after thirty years of living for God, that I find I need the power of God to get out of me. I've been trying to get it out of me, but I guess I'm hiding it behind some door somewhere and every once in a while something blows up and, whew, we're going to have a power blast now, but it isn't going to be the Holy Ghost.

(41) "And Jesus, moved with compassion, put forth his hand, and touched him, and saith unto him, I will, be thou clean. (42) And as soon as he had spoken, immediately the leprosy departed from him, and he was cleansed." Power Encounters. Jesus represented the Kingdom of God, He challenged the kingdom of evil, but He always silenced evil and He always set the captives free.

Power encounters—the first emancipation. God uses Moses to have a power encounter with the magicians. It wasn't talk. If we would have tried to get the Jews out of Israel, we would have went with a debate. "Let me prove it to you by the scriptures." "No, prove it to me by the power." Let me tell you something: pagans, Islamic people, Muslims, Jehovah Witnesses, Mormons, they all have scriptures. So what makes you better? Is your interpretation better? Show me the power. You got sent over somewhere to a pagan, heathen country like Orlando...and see if you can convince the pagan and the heathen and the prostitute and the immoral just from words...but you walk in when their child is sick...or they have a headache or a disease and God gives them a power encounter...now you got validity to what you are talking about.

Power encounter; Moses, magicians. Power encounter; Samson, Philistines. Power encounter; Goliath, David. Power encounter; God, Red Sea. Power encounter; Ark of the Covenant, Israel's priest, Jordan River. Power encounter; Walls of Jericho, shouting. Power encounter; Prophets of Baal, one preacher. "Let the God that answers by fire, let him be God." It is well spoken. Let the demonstration decide.

1 Kings 18:36, watch what he says: "Let it be known this day...that I am thy servant, and that I have done all these

things at thy word." Now that is the difference between a power encounter and tempting God to validate your position. God told him to do that. Well, what has God told you? I read in the beginning of the Bible study Mark 16, "Go into all the world preach the gospel to every creature. He that believes and is baptized shall be saved and he that believeth not shall be damned. These signs shall follow them that believe, heal the sick, cast out devils, take up serpents, drink any deadly thing and it shall not hurt them. Then he went everywhere preaching."

You see, that's our problem. He said…"and these signs shall follow them." You can't follow a parked car. You can't follow a bunch of saints sitting on their duffs doing nothing. Signs won't follow people who aren't attempting to do something. "…These sign shall follow!" That means that somebody ahead is moving.

I prayed for about 46 people at a nearby church last Sunday night. I was rejoicing and was thrilled when I was told today that 2 people got totally healed. What about the 44? I don't know about the 44! I didn't heal the 2! Well aren't you going to get depressed and get drunk tonight? No, it ain't my fault. I can't heal the 44 any more than I can heal the 2. I preached the Gospel and prayed the prayer of faith; you got to believe God heals everybody. Don't take my picture. Don't ask for my autograph. "It's not by might, it's not by power, but it's by my Spirit saith the Lord." God's got to get the glory.

The demonstration that Elijah did with the fire falling…the demonstration…the power encounter. It delivered the duped people. It destroyed and defeated the fake religion. The demonstration, the power encounter, honored God and let God be reinstated as their God.

Daniel 3:26-28, "Then Nebuchadnezzar came near to the mouth of the burning fiery furnace, and spake, and said, Shadrach, Meshach, and Abednego, ye servants of the most high God, come forth, and come hither. Then Shadrach, Meshach, and Abednego, came forth of the midst of the fire. (27) And the princes, governors, and captains, and the king's counsellors, being gathered together, saw these men, upon whose bodies the fire had no power, nor was an hair of their head singed, neither were their coats changed, nor the smell of fire had passed on them.
(28) Then Nebuchadnezzar spake, and said, Blessed be the God..." Whoa! You want to get a pagan to start praising Jehovah? Let him have a power encounter. Let God show up, show off, and show out.

Are you willing to get put into something you can't get out of, so God can get you out? Put them in the fire and couldn't burn them and put...couldn't make them bend. Couldn't make them bow and couldn't change their convictions, and finally the pagans said, "Wow, man, that statue I built is a hill of beans, the one they're serving, man, He's got power. He's got power over fire, and king's decrees, over everything I've tried. I'm a pagan and they're the worshippers of the true living God. Hey Shadrach, Meshach and Abednego, come on out of that fire." And they walk out and he says, "I make a decree" ...a pagan, heathen, and barbarian at heart, "I make a decree; anyone talks bad about their God they're out of here, bud. I'll make your house like a dunghill and kill everything you got. I'll burn you to the ground and you'll be an ashtray."

"When did you get converted?"

"I'm not converted, I just had a power encounter and I just realized their God IS God."

You see, they tried to teach him with their discipline and their lifestyle and, even, maybe quoting scriptures, but it didn't work. But when they had a power encounter, all of a sudden the pagan says, "He's God, no argument from me."

Chapter 6, Verse 20, "And when he came to the den, he cried with a lamentable voice unto Daniel: and the king spake and said to Daniel, O Daniel, servant of the living God, is thy God, whom thou servest continually, able to deliver thee from the lions? (21) Then said Daniel unto the king, O king, live for ever. (22) My God hath sent his angel, and hath shut the lions' mouths, that they have not hurt me: forasmuch as before him innocency was found in me; and also before thee, O king, have I done no hurt. (23) Then was the king exceeding glad for him, and commanded that they should take Daniel up out of the den. So Daniel was taken up out of the den, and no manner of hurt was found upon him, because he believed in his God. (24) And the king commanded, and they brought those men which had accused Daniel, and they cast them into the den of lions..."

You don't have to fuss and cuss with your enemies. You just walk with God and let God give you a power demonstration, and when God sees fit to do it, He'll put them in the fire. (25) "Then King Darius wrote unto all people, nations, and languages, that dwell in all the earth; Peace be multiplied unto you. (26) I make a decree, That in every dominion of my kingdom men tremble and fear before the God of Daniel: for he is the living God, and steadfast for ever, and his kingdom that which shall not be destroyed, and his dominion shall be even unto the end. (27) He delivereth and rescueth, and worketh signs and wonders in heaven and in earth, who has delivered Daniel from the power of the lions."

You know why he's saying all that stuff? He's just had a living, visual, real experience of a power encounter with another world. Don't you get it? When the Lord turned around and said, "I'm going to forgive your sins", that's a power encounter. When you get baptized in Jesus' name, that's a power encounter—the power of the blood and the name. When you get the baptism of the Holy Ghost supernaturally talking in tongues, that's a power encounter. Anybody ever been healed or touched by God? That's a power encounter. The only reason we're blasé and mediocre and apathetic is there's too much distance between the encounters. We have got to diminish the distance between the encounters, so that it starts to become daily.

CHAPTER TWO
Ye men of Israel, hear these words

Acts 2:22, "Ye men of Israel, hear these words; Jesus of Nazareth, a man approved of God among you by miracles and wonders and signs, which God did by him in the midst of you, as ye yourselves also know: (23) Him, being delivered by the determinate counsel and foreknowledge of God, ye have taken, and by wicked hands have crucified and slain." Now, get what this is saying. Now Jesus came with the purpose of dying, but I want you to get this; stepping into the miraculous and the supernatural does not stop Hell from hating you nor attacking. And there's lots of people that'll see all kinds of miracles happen and they still won't believe it. 'Cause the people that crucified Jesus—He had healed a bunch of their people. Okay, are you ready? Acts 2:24, "Whom God hath raised up, having loosed the pains of death: because it was not possible that he should be holden of it."

Luke 10:1, "After these things the Lord appointed other seventy also, and sent them two and two before His face into every city and place, whither he himself would come. (2) Therefore said he unto them, The harvest truly is great, but the labourers are few: pray ye therefore the Lord of the harvest," this is the same thing He said to them way back in Matthew 9:37&38. (2) "...that he would send forth labourers into his harvest. (3) Go your ways: behold, I send you forth as lambs among wolves." Powerful lambs, but still lambs. (4) "Carry neither purse, nor scrip, nor shoes: and salute no man by the way. (5) And into whatsoever house ye enter, first say, Peace be to this house. (6) And if the son of peace be there, your peace shall rest upon it: if not, it shall turn to you again. (7) And in the same house remain, eating and drinking such things as they give: for the labourer is worthy of his hire. Go not from house to house. (8) And into whatsoever city ye enter, and they receive you, eat such things as are set before you:..." watch; (9) "...And heal the sick that are therein, and say unto them, The kingdom of God is come nigh unto you." Every time the Lord uses that term "the kingdom of God," it always has attached with it wonders, signs, miracles, deliverance.

Okay, go a little further in the same chapter. (16) "He that heareth you heareth me;" now, this is going to hurt some people. I don't mean to do this. I can't make Jesus change what He said. It's kind of in the print here. Watch; "He that heareth you heareth me." Now, God is talking about delegated authority and delegated positions and postures of leadership that He puts in the church. And He says, "Now, he that hears you hears me." We got a whole bunch of loonies around this city...many used to attend this church...they think Jesus is lying. No, no. They think they don't have to hear from anyone...you jerk. They say, "I hear from God myself." You won't find any scripture for that. "He that heareth you heareth me." Now watch this; (16) "...and he that despiseth you despiseth me," We got lots of folks who hate the preacher and hate the church. They say, "I love Jesus." Lying dog. You're going to love God you haven't seen, and not love folks you have seen? Ain't going to work. Stay with me, (16) "And he that despiseth me despiseth him that sent me."

See, the whole thing is a chain of command and a chain reaction, so when you look at Ephesians 4:11, ...and God gives apostles, the prophets, the evangelists, the pastors, and teachers, as a gift to the church for the perfecting of the saints, the work of the ministry, the edifying of the body, 'til we all come into a stature of a perfect man...the fullness of man; God is saying, "Listen fellows, I went away on a cloud. I'm leaving leadership here. Be careful how you treat them." Because it's the same thing that God told Moses in Exodus Chapter 33 when He got really angry about their foolishness. God said that; ...I'm not coming among you no more, lest I destroy everybody in the camp, so I'm going to send my angel to go lead you.... Now watch what He says; (Chapter 23:21) ...beware of him, for my name is in him and he will not pardon your folly.... In other words, when an angel does something, buddy, it's just right or just wrong—no mercy. He's a protector and projector of God's holiness, right or wrong—no mercy. And God says, "Don't treat him like you treated Moses." He says; "You tick this boy off and he'll kill everything in your house—and he represents me."

Man, that's why Israel was terrified about God, because the God they dealt with wasn't joking. That's why they didn't even want to get next to Mt. Sinai. When Moses walked up, they said, "That man's crazy, I ain't going up there." That's why they said, "You let Him tell you whatever He has to say, and we'll do what He says, but we ain't getting near Him." They were afraid of Him. But you see, God's sternness with Israel was because they came out of idolatry and immorality and four hundred years of a civilization that was so demented and so perverted that they thought religiosity was 'anything that goes'. And God had to come to them with a stern rebuttal and give them a total turnaround, because their mind set was so whacked out.

Thank God, that God in His tender mercy has come to us incarnated in Jesus of Nazareth. But don't think He's lost His anger or His wrath. And don't think that He's not pursuing holiness and wanting us to live Godly. And He turns around in His kindness and says; "Here, I give you some preachers to help you, but be careful, if you despise him you despise me, if you reject him, you reject me." Why? "Because He's my ambassador just like He said," 'As

I was with Moses so shall I be with you Joshua'." Watch; "As I was with Paul and Peter and the apostles, so will I be with my modern-day ministry." That doesn't mean just me, that means all of us. We're all ministers of the body of Christ.

One more verse. Luke 10:17-19, "And the seventy returned again with joy," wonder how you can get joy out of all that? "...saying, Lord, even the devils are subject unto us through thy name. (18) And he said unto them, I beheld Satan as lightning fall from heaven. (19) Behold, I give unto you power to tread on serpents and scorpions, and over all the power of the enemy:" I really wish you'd underline this, or read this again when you get home, because I think this is the biggest hindrance that we are having right now—"I give you power" (19) "...over all the power of the enemy: and nothing shall by any means hurt you." The reason why we don't deal more with devils is because God knows most of this church is afraid of them.

I'd like you to turn over to Acts 8, Verse 5. I want to continue in this realm of Power Encounters, because I really think that that's the only way we are going to somehow win some people out of this. You're not going to talk people out of this. The draw of flesh is stronger than the draw of Spirit to a person who's unregenerate. You ask anybody if they want to go whoring around Saturday night and drinking and honky-tonkin' and messin' around, or, "You want to go pray"? See what your response will be. In fact, you can ask the same thing to the church people. Not the drinking and whoring around, but, "Would you rather go watch a movie and stay home and fat-cat and eat pizza, or let's go to a prayer meeting"? Ninety percent of this church wouldn't come to pray. We don't understand what's going on. We are being lulled to sleep. You know why? The news media barrages us all day and all night until you get almost inundated with it.   And it's like...like the other day I walked into the barber shop and I said, "You know this thing in Baghdad is really bothering me." It's the way it was when Vietnam was going on, six o'clock news, you just watch people get shot and say, "Oh well, what time is Jackie Gleason coming on?" And every day it's, "Well, two more are shot, one guy blew up, six guys blew up, they blew up ten Jews, they just killed three Israelite's, they killed five Palestinians, and hey, we got a new show on tonight at nine o'clock." And it's like it's no big deal, because tragedy, like sin, has a way of expanding your tolerance until it reaches a level of numbness.

Point in case: when I was a boy...probably the most terrifying films that I ever saw as a kid was Rin Tin Tin—a dog biting somebody, or Trigger, or Roy Rogers, or Dale Evans, or Royal Mounted Police, Sky King, and all those guys. There was no such thing as "damn" and "hell." I mean, they didn't even use those two words. Now...it's okay.

The early apostolic church was not merely a movement, nor was it an organization. It was a walking incarnation of spiritual energy and power. It was a walking incarnation of dynamic, spiritual, other-world power. It was so powerful that even though the world attacked it, the world stood in awe of it. The world feared it. When the world went to arrest its preachers, they didn't send one deputy with a pea shooter, they sent twenty and thirty and forty soldiers and chariots and spearmen and horsemen. When they locked up one unemployed preacher named Simon Peter, the Bible said that they chained him to a wall with four quaternions of soldiers – that's sixteen soldiers – and they put him in the inner prison and chained him to the wall and put a guard on the outside. Now, who's afraid of who? I mean, he's just an unemployed preacher. He doesn't have a .357 Magnum, he don't have nothing. Why don't you just go up and tell him you're the Big Bad Wolf and surrender?

It's the same kind of thing that happened...remember the story of Sampson in the Book of Judges, when Sampson will not put up with the rest of the church people that Israel's putting up with? The Philistines are invading them. They're molesting their woman, they're stealing their groceries, they're robbing their land, and they're just lying back..., "Oh, well, what can we do?" Well, Sampson gets really ticked and says, "Well, let's kill everything we can, that's what we can do." And Sampson gets anointed with the power of God and he starts bashing in skulls, he starts burning fields down with putting a hundred fox tails together, he starts attacking everything he can find, the Spirit of God is moving on him to attack and fight the Midianites. He's resisting them. Guess what happens? He has destroyed so many thousands of them that they're afraid of one guy! Guess how they get him? They go to the church and say, "Could you betray your brother to us?" I'm in the Bible; we're the New Testament Church. Israel is the Old Testament Church. And they went to Israel and said, "You know, we can't get a hold of this guy. This is a bad dude here. But now, you're his brethren. You get him to surrender." And the Bible says he goes up to the rock Etam. Sitting up on the rock, he's looking down at everybody, and here comes a few thousand Israelites. One guy—no weapons. Who's afraid of who? See, carnal people are always afraid of spiritual people. It has nothing to do with us; I was just making a statement.

And they come up and he say's, "What are you doing?"

They say, "We've come up to bind you, Sampson."

"But I'm your brother."

"Yeah, but you're causing a lot of grief here, man. You're busting skulls and killing people and you're tickin' them Midianites off. We've come up with a better program than separation and holiness. Come on. Conformity to the world, acquiescence to their concepts, live by their lifestyles, peaceful co-existence at any price."

And Sampson said, "Not hardly."

They said, "We've come up."

And before Sampson would fight against his brethren...because he could kill them backslidden dirtbags as easily as he could the Philistines...he said, "Promise me that you won't fall upon me yourself." Now, he wasn't afraid they would kill him, he was afraid that if they attacked him, the power of God would come on him and he'd clean the house. So he said, "You promise me you won't attack me and I'll come peaceful."

And they said, "We won't attack you, we'll just deliver you to our enemies."

Jesus have mercy, sounds like Judas and Jesus. It sounds like the Jews..., "Well, we've got to kill Jesus, but not on a High day. You know, it's church." They're ready to go in and take Jesus to get him crucified and murdered, and they say, "We can't come into Pilot's hall, it's a High day." Got murder in their heart, but they don't want to walk on a Gentile's rug.

So, they deliver Sampson...we know the story. And they start yelling at Lehi, laughing and jumping. The Bible says, "They began to shout and rejoice to their god, Dagon, because Dagon had delivered." Yeah, he delivered them alright. "Delivered him into our hands." I always thought that was so funny. The minute the Philistines shouted, the power hit Sampson. Ha-ha, I like that. Sampson's just standing there minding his own business and these morons start shouting, which proves to me that people without the Spirit can shout; means that people in false doctrine can put on a show.

They just wrote my article up in the new Pentecostal Herald. It was kind of neat, had my picture up there and everything. And I have an article there on worship. And one of the bottom lines it says I said, "The only difference between Oneness Pentecostal worship and charismatic cowboy worship is one subject: Truth." That is the thing that gives worship its power; truth. Because the charismatic people are just as sincere as the Pentecostal people, the difference is truth. And the difference of the outcome of all worship and service will always be your object. As long as we keep Jesus as the object of our worship, and not our feelings and not our emotions and not goose bumps, we're going to have a great outcome.

Well, the story said the power of God hit Sampson and he killed a thousand with a jawbone of a donkey. That ain't bad for a day's work. Then he just threw away that jawbone. I preached before on that: Picked It Back Up and Got a Drink." Ain't got nothing to do with my Bible study, I'm just wandering, 'cause I'm trying to feel your temperature. Well, I'm going to repent; it does have something to do with my Bible study. Everything I just told you is about a spiritual encounter. In Sampson, when the power of God hit him, it was a power encounter between the truth and the false.

Sometimes you don't want to...I don't believe one time that Sampson was premeditating crushing a thousand skulls, but the Spirit of God came on him, which is the Spirit of Truth, and Truth went after false. And the problem we have is that when you have a real power encounter, you cannot control it. It can get absolutely messy. That's why even in Pentecostal churches we don't want a lot of power encounters. We like the church governed and simple and, "It's twenty-five after, I hope he's finished by nine, I got things to do." But if the Holy Ghost starts falling or devils start walking in, the majority of this church says, "I'm out of here, pal." Why? "I don't like that power encounter stuff. I substitute power encounter for concept and ideology and thought." But everything that ever happened in these scriptures that was monumental, that helped the people of God, Old and New Testament, was always the result of a power encounter.

It's the Kingdom of God against the kingdom of Satan. It's the power of one kingdom versus the power of the other kingdom. That's why Paul got angry when he wrote his epistle to that church...bunch of whoremongers and drunks and worldly, ungodly people. Yeah, they had the Holy Ghost. Yeah, they were baptized in Jesus' name. But they were vile and they were wicked and they needed to be disciplined; they needed to be taught. That's why you don't get everything when you get the baptism of the Holy Ghost. You don't get everything when you step into the baptismal tank. That's why God has ordained preaching and teaching and discipleship and helping people, because the Holy Ghost doesn't do everything for you.

So they had a power encounter–power of Samson's God against the power of Baal Dagon. Even when they captured the Ark of the Covenant they took it in the house of Dagon. Remember the story? I think it's in, about, Judges Chapter 5. They put it in the temple. Remember that? Dumbest thing. Dumbest thing you can ever do is put truth with error. Why? Error's going to fall. They got up in the morning...man...poor old Dagon's all lying out on the ground. He's all messed up. He got his head knocked off. They picked him back up. Can you imagine being a worshiper of a god that just got his head knocked off? And you put it back up..., "Man, I'm sorry. I hope you feel better today." And your god's head is hangin' on the floor and you got the dumb stump over here. And the next day, God just slaps it down on the ground and then cut off his palms and his hands and his arms....now it's just a stub up there. You're going to bow down and worship that? That's as dumb as worshipping a five hundred pound Buddha, with his belly hanging clear down to his knees. What's a matter with you people? Don't you get it? Folks, it was a power encounter. The Ark of the Covenant was symbolic of God's presence. He took it as an insult to put Him next to this false image, so God just slapped him down.

Let me try it again. The early church was more than a movement, and it was not just an organization. A walking incarnation of spiritual energy—that's what I want for my life. I don't want to just be a church junkie. I want to be a bad-hair day to Hell every day that I get up. I want to get up and Hell says, "Oh, God, I wish he'd go someplace else." Now, I know you smile and laugh and you think, "Poor Arnie's a sick man, he needs help." Well, when you get up in the morning, what does Hell think about you? "Ain't no big deal...I could put their prayer life in a whiskey thimble and have three inches left." I want to get up in the morning and say, "Well, it's me and you again, bubba." Everyday I get up I'm expecting some kind of confrontation. I'm either going to receive one, or I'm going to cause one. I have a feeling you people are like that slick Willy guy. They put that slick Teflon stuff on you saints. You're the Teflon saints. You just slide through everything. Nothing ever touches you. You can pass two hundred people a day, they'd never know you were a Christian, 'cause you got that Teflon stuff. Okay. All together; ready? Let's look at the floor....

Everywhere Jesus went He was a power encounter. Let me tell you, He didn't go looking for trouble. He was Truth, He was Life, He was the love of God in a body. He wasn't filled with hate and animosity towards people. He hated evil. He hated wickedness. He hated what sin and sickness and demon possession was doing to people. He didn't hate the people. We have no right to hate the people. We need to love the people. But understand that Paul says in Ephesians, "For we wrestle not against flesh and blood, but against principalities, and powers, and spiritual wickedness in high places." We're wrestling against these powers that are birthing all this kind of stuff. Don't you get it? Hell needs bodies just like Heaven needs bodies. Hell needs ambassadors; Heaven needs ambassadors. That's why the Book says, "And you are the body of Christ, you are God's building, you are God's house, you are God's bride, you are God's called out one, His ecclesia, you are His Church. You were called out of darkness, brought into light to show forth the praises of Him who did that for you." You need to be a living demonstration against evil. Not with words, but with power.

When Paul wrote to that church with all their drunkenness, orgies, and immorality...read it...he says, "I'm going to come to you this next time..." read it. The man's hurting. He's just a man, though he's an apostle. He says, "I'm going to come to you this next time, because I've heard about your people in your church that say, 'I ain't nothing', that jerk ain't nothing, he's an idiot, his bodily presence is sick, his speech is contemptible'." Paul says, "I've heard what you've said about me. Fine, I'm going to come and then I'm going to contend with all the people in your congregation. And we're going to see who has the power."

Now see, Paul says; "Yeah, my speech is contemptible. I'm a little frail in body, right. I'm feared with much trembling. But, I have the power of God in my life. And the only reason you're a church is because God used me to birth stuff in you." And Paul said, "I don't mind being insulted by you people, but I'm going to tell you something: How did you get the miraculous and the supernatural in your church? Was it by keeping the law, or was it by the work of faith and the power of the Holy Ghost? For when I came to you, I came not in word, but in demonstration and power of the Holy Ghost, that your faith shouldn't stand in the wisdom of man, but in the power of God."

How was the church in Corinth built? A power encounter. Look...come on. Put your hand on your chest and say, "I'm supposed to be a power house. I'm supposed to give Hell a bad day. Hell doesn't want to see me coming." It's hard for us to accept that. "Well, the preacher, that's why he gets paid eight hundred million dollars a year, that's why he should do that and we should sit and watch TV." I don't think so! We are the body of Christ. Do you realize that we are only as strong as we each are corporately? Look, remember this thing I told you about the Church? The walking incarnation...spiritual energy? It began at Pentecost, with an infusion of power that moved in power. But when the Church began to compromise its standards, its doctrine, its separation with the world around her, the Church began to diminish in power. And when she diminished in power, the Church dug in her heels to try and keep her previous gains. And she was no longer spiritually alive, a living organism, but now she became a fleshly organization. It is our desperate job now that we regain our lost power with God.

Now, the first issue of power was given when we repented and God filled us with the Holy Ghost. But if we are to regain some of the anointing and the power that we've lost over the centuries, we are going to have to seek God for it, or He will not do it. God will let us live at the level of our own luke-warmness. God will let a world that He wants to give the Holy Ghost to be lost forever and go to a devil's Hell before He'll force the Holy Ghost on anybody. As much as He wants to save every precious soul on this planet, six point five billion people, He will not force anybody to love Him, and to serve Him, and to embrace Calvary, and to love the blood, and to step in the water and be filled with the Holy Ghost. He will not force this so-called assembly of His body to live in a high level of divine energy, if we don't want it. He will let us live in the lowlands and the swamps and we'll get a little touch once in awhile, a little tear will come down our eye, talk in tongues maybe, maybe not talk in tongues. And we'll just move through and say, "Well, I didn't smoke and I didn't drink and I didn't do this and I didn't do that," but we have not accomplished what God has left us here to do: It's to reach into the kingdom of Satan and snatch people out of it.

Anybody besides me ever contended with a drunk? I mean, after you got done verbally you got to do something physically. Anybody? Anybody ever contended with your own children physically? Guess what that was? A power encounter. That little tyke, that little darling, he or she thought she had the power, until mom or dad unleashed the power. Then, all of a sudden, there was conversion. That's right. You do the same thing when children go to school. You do the same thing with your employees and employers. There's always power encounters. There's always someone gonna' push the parameters to see how far they'll stretch and how much the person in charge will tolerate. It's all power encounters. Some are on lower levels; some are very high. The highest you can have is spiritual encounters.

The only way you and I can regain our lost power is to return to praying to the Person who first gave us our power. And unless we make contact with Jesus, we're dead meat. The issue is not "believing", the issue is "contact." The issue is grabbing a hold of the horns of the altar until God…it's, somehow, seeking God with a tenacity and a desperation until God lights a flame in our hearts again, until somehow we convulse with a brokenness and a weeping for the lost and the hurting and the suffering of our world. There's no way our children, our loved ones, are coming back to the Kingdom of God with us praying a little prayer like, "Oh Jesus, she needs to be saved, please help her, Amen." That'll never work.

Hell's sitting on the corner just laughing his fool head off at us, because he's pulled all his stops out. I mean, people doing this vile stuff in broad daylight. Doing this stuff on TV and movies and radio and literature. They're not ashamed. I don't understand where the Pentecostal church picked up shame. What are we afraid of? What are we ashamed of? I tell ya; it would be easier for us in this city if there were no other so-called Christian churches. We would have authority. We are intimidated by other denominational believers who are "good people." You need to understand; good people and saved people ain't the same. There is a thing called "entering into the kingdom", that Jesus said, "Except you're born of water and spirit, you can't see the kingdom, you can't enter the kingdom." Now Jesus said that, but this world report says, "Jesus is lying. Jesus doesn't even know what He's talking about. There are no absolutes. What Jesus said, he didn't…." I just read a full report by a guy who's got more degrees than a thermometer…well, he explained that Jesus was borderline crazy, that He didn't really understand what he meant, He was a zealot, and He was just trying to help the Jews, but that has nothing to do with us.

That's the society we're living in. You better get a hold of some absolutes. You better put your anchor of your soul down in something and say, "Come Hell or high water, here's where I stay and I'm not moving from this. This is right if everybody else goes the other way." You got to get something anchored in your soul, because the winds are blowing. And Paul wrote to the Ephesians church that in the last day that the winds of doctrine are going to blow so strong that it's going to blow people right off their moorings, unless they're really solidly anchored.

It's more important for us to have prayer around here than to have preaching. If I announce this Sunday night that I'm not preaching and we're all coming to pray, half of you would stay home and watch TV. It reveals what you think about the Kingdom. When you don't want to pray, you are saying, "I'm as close to God as any man or woman could ever be." "There's not this much between me and the cheek of God." "I'm so close to God it scares me." If we plan on rescuing the perishing and we plan on saving the sinful and helping the sick and the suffering, we must somehow, first be correct in doctrine. We must understand our purpose, and most of all, we must be assured that we have been divinely equipped for the mission, for the issue is spiritual and not intellectual. It is not; "I believe in Jesus." That won't work. I'll tell you what else won't work; "Well, I go to the Pentecostal Church." That won't work either. What'll work is; "Jesus I know and Paul I know and I know you, too." You want criteria for your life? I want to be known in Hell and Heaven at the same time. I want Hell to know my name and I want Hell to fear my fame.

Friend, we need to cause some Hell for some help. We need to create some chaos. We need to bring Heaven to confront people who are on drugs, who are space cadets, who are immoral, who are liars, who are indecent, other people who are moral and decent, but are just fools and deceived and are in false doctrine and wrong churches. We need to look at all this stuff. If you believe that this church teaches the Truth, and everybody around here's not teaching this, then somebody's wrong. You need to go by churches and pray for God to do one of two things: bring them people out of there and bring them here, or the easier way—they already got a building, bring the light of revelation to this place and let these people see Jesus' name baptism and the Holy Ghost and fill this whole place with...what a great city if everybody was filled with the Holy Ghost, baptized in Jesus' name. We'd have to leave here and go somewhere else, because the name of the game is evangelism.

The Book of Acts, tonight, must be rescued from being just a history book. It must again become to us a pulsating, powerful pattern for New Testament Christianity. You don't have any other pattern for New Testament Christianity. Don't listen to this stuff...I'm an ex-southern Baptist; I'm not a virgin voice. I knew Billy Graham before he was famous and I'm one of the kids getting saved at Madison Square Garden, Hillside Roller Rink, Crusade for Christ, Campus for Christ; I got saved at all of those things. And I was sincere and I had some kind of spiritual experience and God did something great in my life...kept me away from being worse than I could have been. I think, each time, it's a progressive step towards the full realization of what you're supposed to do, and even though you want to say, "Well, all those people are lost", well, I thank God for every one of those people who ever taught me a Sunday school lesson, every one that ever picked me up and took me to a Sunday school class, everybody that ever took me to someplace. Man, no telling what I might've done if God hadn't started something in my life there.

I got a divided house here right now. The Bible said Apollos (Acts 18:24) was a mighty man, eloquent in his scriptures, instructed in the way of the Lord...watch...knowing only the baptism of John. But he was a mighty man and he was walking in all the light and all the truth that he had. Apollos bumps into Aquila and Priscilla and they don't do, "Listen you damnable Baptist fool, you're going to go to Hell, you and Billy...." He didn't say that. They heard what he said. They pulled him aside...aside...aside. Why? They're fixin' to have a power encounter. They're going to share the power of revealed truth and supernatural experiences they have and hopefully add it to this man's precious foundation that he already has. And they pull him aside, the Bible says, and they explain unto him the way of the Lord more perfectly. That's all they did. A power encounter. And the next time you hear the name Apollos mentioned, he is mentioned with the two leaders of the Christian church. And he writes in the Corinth epistle, he says, "Some of you say you're of Cephas (that's Peter) and some say you're of Paul and others say you are of Apollos." He's running with the two top dogs, the two apostles. That's how powerful this man was when he got the full revelation.

I wonder how many Apollos' right now are in Gainesville. I wonder how many Cornelius' tonight, are praying for light to come...for truth. I really do! I wonder how many precious Presbyterians and Episcopalians or Lutherans are looking at this thing and "ye shall receive power after the Holy Ghost come", and I wonder if they say, "I wonder if that was for us or that was not for us?" "No, my Pastor says and my Priest says that's not for us." But I think there are thousands of people that pray every day and every night in this city who are hungry to know God in power and in personal realization, rather than in theory.

Now come on, all of us, somewhere in our life, there was a time that we believed in God in theory. There's a big difference in believing in God in theory and bumping into God and getting knocked down. It's kinda' like what Naaman said, "Well, I thought, but now I know." See, there's the difference. He *thought* this was the way the preacher should have done it, but then when he told him to go in the water, he dipped seven times, and when he came back out and he got healed of leprosy he said, "Now I *know*." See, that's where you people are. Thank God. You are in that blessed position, "Now I know." I don't know everything, but I know something. I'm better off than I used to be, I got more power than I used to have, I got more peace than I used to have, there's anointing on me better than I used to have. And I'll say something else; and most of us can probably say, "And I'm not everything I want to be, but considering what I used to be, I'm a lot better now than I used to be and I know that I know, that I know that I know."

We need to become this powerful Christianity. Signs and wonders and miracles are supposed to work in two realms: the physical and the spiritual. Why? Here's why: signs and wonders and miracles, when they work, see, I'm not only talking about healing the sick, I'm talking about helping hurting, emotional, busted up, broken people. You realize God has allowed this generation to be tailor-made to an apostolic church? Never been so many divorces, been so many rapes. Never been so many brutalized spouses, messed up heads, drug addiction everywhere, whacked out people, living under a pressure cooker, working sixty and eighty hours a week, the husband and the wife...they kiss by mail.... You realize that this whole generation is made just right for an apostolic church to come walkin' in and offer people the wonderful, compassionate, merciful message of Jesus Christ and not just a little mindset thing? I mean, you can tell people, "Man, if you'll come, you'll feel the power of God. The Holy Ghost will touch ya.' It will turn your life around. It will bring something to ya'."

There's something about a human testimony. When you talk to somebody, you don't need to know a bunch of scripture, you just need to know Jesus. If you know Jesus, and He's real in your life, when you talk to somebody they are going to sense the quickening reality of the Holy Ghost. We don't need to be debating and fussin' and cussin' and fightin' with a bunch of people. "How much does Daniel's image weigh?" "How far is the moon away...?" "What's the seventieth week in Daniel?" Who gives a rot?! I'm not being disrespectful. It ain't got nothin' to do with us. We're going to be gone. People giving us Excedrin headaches tryin' to find out the seventieth week and the image and who's the beast and the sixty two weeks and the seventy weeks and here comes the sixty nine weeks and Messiah and what if.... You know all that stuff ain't never won a soul, you nincompoop!!! What's that about getting people full of the Holy Ghost? You don't get it yet, what I'm sayin' here: if people don't get full of the Holy Ghost and get baptized in Jesus' name, they're lost. Now, I know we don't believe that, but they're lost. If they're not lost, Jesus didn't tell the truth. Because Jesus said, "Except you're born of water...."

Signs and wonders and miracles for the physical and the spiritual...watch...they are necessary, because they and they alone, alone, alone, give absolute proof that Jesus is alive. Doctrine doesn't give it. Doctrine gives direction for correct living and discipline in life. Supernatural equipment tells you He's alive. That's why Jesus told people, "Go and preach the Gospel of the Kingdom and then heal the sick, cleanse the lepers, cast out devils, raise the dead." Why? "They'll know that I'm alive." Why? 'Cause He was only seen by a handful of 'em. And when they went around saying, "Jesus is alive", they made fun of Paul.

In Acts 17 at the Areopagus, when he went to Mars' hill and he debated and he talked to them about...he's demanded that every man repent for his appointed day when He shall judge the world by that man whom He raised from the dead. And when he said, "Raised from the dead", they laughed him out of the Areopagus and he just left. Why? Because debate won't do it, because the world loves debate. Schwarzenegger's having one right now. Thirty-eight billion dollars in debt in California. Who'd want to govern that bunch of junk? Is that ego, or what? They're debating. Nothing will be settled from the debate. If I was asking a question, I'd say, "Where's the thirty-eight billion? We need it." You hand me thirty-eight billion...you got the power. You hand me promises for thirty-eight billion...you're just a politician. Now, you're laughing.

Okay, let's turn the other way. Jesus saves, Jesus heals, Jesus changes, Jesus transforms...no power—just another bunch of church junkies that dress funny. But let the power – *PHEWW* – bring tears flowing down somebody's face, let their lips begin to quiver and their hands shake and their head...because the Holy Ghost unction starts coming on somebody. They don't know whether they're scared or whether they're happy. They don't know whether to run in or run forward. I'm talking to somebody! You feel the power of another world and that is a power encounter. And even if you don't believe the doctrine, you could never walk out and deny that God has not put His hand on you, that a supernatural something took place that night. Remember the old song? Maybe two of you are old enough to remember it. "I went to a meeting one night." "And my heart wasn't right, but something got a hold of me."

Whatever happened to those "something got a hold of me" meetings we used to have? You know what I think we've done? We've traded them for my preaching. I'm supposed to be preaching, but I'm a very poor substitute for "something got a hold of me." How many more sermons do you need before you start praying?

We have got to offer the world the proof that Jesus is alive. Not only is He alive, but He is totally unchanged in His purpose and His power. The miraculous and the supernatural is nothing more or less than God acting like Himself. The Jesus that used to deliver, delivers. The Jesus that used to fill, fills. The Jesus that used to change lives, changes lives. It's not mental, it's not intellectual, it's supernatural energy that gets inside a man or a woman.

Okay, I'm going to try one more thing; I want to ask you a simple question. I really have a great Bible study...I mean, I've only talked to you from the restaurant check paper here. This little thing is all I talked on. I really have a good one over here, but I just can't seem to get to it. I'm trying to talk about power encounters and I can't get past first base here. Let me ask you a simple question: If Jesus Christ manifested Himself right now, standing right there, right there, He manifested Himself right now, so you can see him...here's the question; what would He do about the situation, the sinner, or the sick person? 'Cause if you don't make up your mind on this, you don't even know what you're doing.

What would Jesus do?

We always blow off Hebrews 13:8; "Jesus Christ the same yesterday, and to day, and for ever." Malachi 3:6; "For I am the LORD, I change not." We hoop and holler, but every time I want to ask that question...if He was right here, what would He do if you presented your situation to Him? How would He act to you regarding your sickness, or your pain, or your disease, or your sorrow, or your brokenness, or your home life, or the problems you're having emotionally? What would He do? You must answer it! Would He deny? Would He delay? Or would He deliver? That's what you have to answer. 'Cause that's why everything is happening—that's why people come here. They're coming not to get another delay. Say, "Oh, you should have been here last Sunday, boy, we had good church last Sunday, but God's not in town tonight, He's in Puerto Rico tonight, He'll be in Bangladesh on Tuesday, you come a week from Wednesday I think He's going to swing through here." Would He liberate the person, or would He lecture to the person on how they're learning, or how much He loves them while cancer's eating their head off? Would He ignore them, saying, "You know, I've got to go talk to the University of Florida tonight." Or would He turn around and help them? Now, only you can answer that. And your mindset, combined with mine, will set the temperature of these services. And we see people come in here and they're all whacked out, they're broken-hearted, they've got problems, or maybe they're fidgety or what-have-you...if you could release your faith and mindset that, "Oooh, if Jesus was here right now, He'd help this person, He'd fix this situation, He'd come to their rescue..." You realize how much potential is in this house right now, of faith that could be released in this house?

Please don't be offended at me. I'm not mad, I'm not rude.

I'm just saying that I was a powerless Baptist. My mother and all my aunts and me, for awhile, as a child, were powerless Roman Catholics. Then I became a powerless Presbyterian. Then I went to the Church of God, then I went to the Four Square Church, then I went to the Nazarene church. It was always powerless. I always believed what they said was right. I always believed that the moral principals that they taught were right and that Jesus died for me and that I should live a better life. But, I never had a power encounter.

And I could never overcome the power encounter that I would face when I left the church. I'd get allured into a honky-tonk and go out drinking and get drunk. I'd live like a stupid fool. There was a power that was drawing me and seducing me and moving me that I had nothing to resist. I would try to resist it in my mind saying, "No, Jesus doesn't want me to do this." But it wasn't enough because, you see, intellectual mind power is not even in the same ball park with spiritual power.

What do you think all this Harry Potter stuff is? You understand what this is? This is a quest by people. Now, they don't think it's witchcraft, although it's witchcraft, they think it's just neat to learn how to cast spells and be able to hurt people and be able to make people do your stuff. That's control, that's a power encounter. That's what the world is wanting. But they're going about it the wrong way and we're here to try to tell people there's a better way to touch power.

I hope that one good seed, maybe, has got into somebody's heart and maybe you will go pray about it awhile, mull it over in you spirit, maybe you will just say, "You know what, I just need the power of God in my life." Lord, I want the power of God. And I know I have to go through valleys and struggles and there's dry seasons and there's troubles and problems, but there is always joy and victory. And I know that you've never ordained anybody to live twenty four seven on top of the mountain because the chaos and the trouble and the problem hurting people, they live in the valley. But I do thank you for trips and journeys to the mountaintop, for a refreshing and a renewing. I thank you, that the bush still burns tonight and like Moses of old, we too can be illuminated and energized and helped.

I pray for that wonderful treatment that you gave in the book of Jude, to praying in the Holy Ghost, renewing myself in the Holy Ghost. You said, there would come a generation in the last day, sensual, having not the Spirit. Lord, I don't want to be that. I don't want to be a plastic Pentecostal. I don't want to be what Paul wrote to Timothy: having a form and denying the power thereof. I'm asking you to help us as a church family to become so hungry and thirsty and prayerful and careful in seeking your face, that we could somehow find the joy and the fulfillment of impacting people for your name's sake. You've been so good to us and we're grateful and we're debtors to you.

CHAPTER THREE
Unpracticed truth is no better than false doctrine

I have something written on the front of my Bible with my 42 or 43 different paper clips and I refer to it often. It says, "Unpracticed truth is no better than false doctrine." The person who has a book and doesn't read it is no better than a blind person. A person who can play a musical instrument and doesn't do it might as well have no hands. I got another one I want to say to you: The popularity and acceptance of false doctrine in America will never change a lie into the truth. I don't care what the government says about moral issues, when God went on record a long time ago and said, "This is moral and this is immoral." It doesn't matter how much adjudication takes place, how many things the Supreme Court justices do—God will not change His opinion for our opinion.

When God goes on record we need to grab it, because He's absolutely, totally wise. He's absolute, total knowledge. And He's totally and absolutely good, so if He gives us any declaration, it's the best thing that could ever come down the pike. It's not up for being amended; it's not up for debate. You know...God turns around; He doesn't debate anybody. In fact, He doesn't even debate His own existence; He just comes out and says, "I am." He let's all the dingbats try to debate where He came from, and He goes, "No, no! I am—That's enough." I like that. I like that! One translator says in the Hebrew, when it says, 'I am', it says, "I am the becoming one, because I am that already and I am becoming anything you need me to do in time."

Acts 2:22, it's getting to be a favorite verse of mine. "Ye

men of Israel, hear these words; Jesus of Nazareth, a man approved of God among you by miracles and wonders and signs, which God did by him in the midst of you, as ye yourselves also know:" A man approved of God how? "...by miracles, wonders, and signs." I've taught you for months now; those were Jesus' credentials. He said that if you don't believe my words, he said...believe my works that you might believe my words because my works validate my words. That's the grand blessing of the resurrection. When Jesus got up out of the dirt He said; ...everything I said before I went into the dirt was right, ain't it...? You see, that's why the Bible said that God raised the awesome power of holiness that was displayed by God. When He raised Him from the dead, He upset the whole underworld. He wrecked the whole joint; He tore the place in two. I don't think we've ever understood what happened. When Jesus came out of the grave, before He could get out of the grave, He had to get out of the bowels of the Earth.

Ephesians 4 said; ...He that ascended, first descended into the lower parts of the Earth..... He wrecked Hell. He gave them a bad hair day. It ain't ever been the same since. He snapped chains, He broke off shackles, He raised the righteous dead out of the abyss from below, brought 'em up after His resurrection, took the keys of death and Hell out of Satan's hand and said; You ain't in charge no more, and don't blow no smoke at nobody. You gotta grab a hold of that, because the resurrection is the validation of what you have. That's why we preach the baptism of the Holy Ghost, 'cause the baptism of the Holy Ghost is resurrecting power. The same power that raised Jesus from the dead, new-birthed people into the Kingdom. The Holy Ghost is the resurrector.

I want to go back in the Book of Luke. I just know we're right there and we just gotta keep pushing and pushing. I just don't want you to feel like, "Oh God, another message on miracles. I'm so sick of it." You wouldn't be if you got a miracle! That's like some people saying, "I wish we could hear something better than preaching on the Holy Ghost." You wouldn't say that if you just got the Holy Ghost!

Luke 10:1, "After these things the Lord appointed other seventy also, and sent them two and two before his face into every city and place, whither he himself would come." Boy, I'd like to preach a sermon on that sometime: "I'm set ahead of Him; He's coming right behind me." It was like those disciples were sent out and said, "I'm not the big show, I'm just the barker. The King's coming right behind me." You didn't hear what I just said: God sends you into situations, not so that you can feel alone, but that you could realize that right behind you...He's coming. So if it doesn't happen when I pray for you, don't worry about it, He's just around the bend. He's fixin' to validate this. It said He sent them two by two before every place He, Himself, would come. It's like He said; "Don't worry, I'll catch up to you after a while." Sometimes, I think He's lost my address, but He knows where I am.

Verse 2, "Therefore said he unto them, The harvest truly is great, but the labourers are few: pray ye therefore the Lord of the harvest, that he would send forth labourers into his harvest." It's the same thing He told the other fellows in Matthew 10. And then He tells them different things; to go into peoples' houses; but I read this again this morning and it just leapt out at me. Verse 3, "Go your ways: behold, I send you forth as lambs among wolves." ...Go your ways: behold, I send you into a disadvantaged position. You got to read that in the NIV, the "Nearly Inspired Version...." He says...now this doesn't seem fair when I read this: "Behold I send you forth as lambs among wolves." Now that ain't fair. Now, "gorillas among wolves", I could take it. "King Kong among kitty cats", I can take it. But He says; ...I am sending you in the posture and nature of a lamb and I'm putting you among the wolves...you better hope I'm coming right behind you. You see, that's why He said it. He said; ...It's two by two and every place which He, Himself, would come.... Why? 'Cause He's sending you into wolves and He says; ...You're like lambs and the lamb ain't got a chance against a wolf.... It can't outrun the wolf, he doesn't have fangs, he doesn't have a claws. A lamb can die within 100 yards of water, 'cause they don't smell well. A lamb can die, they call it being cast, a lamb will lay over on its side and when it wants to scratch its back, a lamb will roll on its back, it loses its equilibrium and lambs die on their back unless the shepherd shows up. What is He saying? ...You better stay close to the shepherd.

Verse 9, "And heal the sick that are therein, and say unto them, the Kingdom of God is come nigh unto you." Apparently the miraculous is an indicator and evidence of the Kingdom of God. See, we've made the Kingdom of God our talk, we've made the Kingdom of God our hairdos, dress codes, don't play putt-putt golf, don't wear cufflinks. But the Kingdom of God is a demonstration of supernatural power dealing with other powers.

Then He goes a little bit further; He warns these people in Verse 13, "Woe unto thee, Chorazin! woe unto thee, Bethsaida! for if the mighty works had been done in Tyre and Sidon, which have been in you, they had a great while ago repented, sitting in sackcloth and ashes." Now here's the key, He's giving you the key in Verse 13: The purpose of the miraculous in two-fold; 1) to alleviate suffering, sorrow, pain, bondage, hostage holding; 2) it set the platform so that people will repent. He said that if the great, mighty works had been done in you, they would have repented long ago. Well, they weren't preaching repentance, they were preaching the delivering power of God. Yeah, but when you preach the delivering power of God, and God delivers them, God expects a thankful spirit to come out of your heart and say, "God save me, a sinner man, I ain't right, I need help."

There's another purpose of healing, and I think we need to grab a hold of it. It's found in the Gospel of John, Chapter 9. It's the man who was born blind. And the debate comes...the theologians talking about how come he was born blind...blah blah blah...it was his mother's and father's sin...did he sin...? No, no, no...let the works of God be manifested in his life...and He spits on him! Boy, that'll kill your pride. The Bible said that He made spittle and just put that yucky stuff right on this guy's eyeballs and then told him to go wash in the pool of Siloam. I've often thought that was a strange request to tell a blind man;

"Now go wash in the pool of Siloam."

"Sure, I'll be glad to. Could you just point me in the general direction?"

Think about it. Sometimes we read and gloss over stuff: "Command you right now...." You're here...and the Lord Jesus appears in a glorified body, puts a big whopper on the floor, picks up some dust and throws it on your eyeballs and says, "I want you to wash at the YMCA pool over there on 34th Street, get on down there." How are you going to find 34th Street? You can't even find the back of the church! Now see. Watch what He's trying to show you: If God doesn't use you immediately to heal the sick, He may just use you to help the sick find the place.

In Matthew 9:27-30; remember the story of the two blind men and they cried unto Jesus and He ignored 'em? And they kept crying unto Jesus and He went into the house and the Bible says when He would come in the house they'd come to him. How did they find the house? They're blind! Unless the people that could see...that knew where Jesus was...went out of their way, turned off their TV and said, "Yeah, I'll show you where He is." Why would God use any of us in the supernatural and the miraculous and the direct healing ministry when we won't help folks that can't see? "Use me Lord!" There's 400 people around you. Open the door for somebody, give them a ride, give them some direction.

Come on, watch this; Luke 10:16, "He that heareth you heareth me, he that despiseth you despiseth me, and he that despiseth me despiseth him that sent me." It's kind of like a ladder of progression. (17) And the seventy returned again with joy, saying, Lord, even the devils are subject unto us through thy name." They didn't even have the Holy Ghost. Jesus has not yet been glorified. John 7:37-39. Calvary hasn't happened. Resurrection hasn't taken place. Ascension and descension have not happened. He has just given them, by faith and by sovereign choice, power, anointing, and enablement. And devils are subject unto them through His name. Well, what ought to happen with us? We got the power!

Let me tell you something friends; just because you talked in tongues doesn't mean you got power. Talking in tongues is the evidence of the reception of the Holy Ghost. That's without debate Acts 2, Acts 8, Acts 9, Acts 10, Acts 19. That's finished. But the issue is the indwelling and the communion and the union of my spirit with God's, because some of us, I think, are trying to live in a present-day conflict with yesterday's goo-goo stuff. "...Well, I talked in tongues in 1974...." That's great. See, there needs to be a renewal. That's why we need a prayer life. That's why we need to make constant contact with God. You're lookin' at me like I'm crazy, but what kind of marriage would you have if you kissed her once on the wedding day and from then on you shook hands? And then after about 5 years you grunted from behind the paper. No roses, no candy, no gifts, no kind words, you just hold up your paper, "We're married, get off my back." Now, you're smiling, because that's ignorant, I mean, that analogy is crazy. How many times have I told you: People that have lousy marriages, that have no romance, no intimacy, no kindness, no interaction, and then try to prove that "I love you", ...I bought you a washing machine last year, what do you want? And I got you a dryer, too! What do you want, a self-propelled lawn mower? ...Bought you a dishwasher.... Uh oh.

When I was younger, my mom didn't have a...what do you call that thing...uh, an egg beater thing. She used to make me take it, it was on a little thing with a little mesh thing and we used to mash the potatoes with that strainer thing. Does anybody remember that? We didn't have any money, we had a scrub board that was in the tub and we used to scrub the.... Ha, my mother was the washing machine! Can you imagine washing all day, working all day, your hands all shriveled up, and her husband comes home and says, "Of course I love you, here's a giant box of Fab, saved you a trip to the store." I mean it's so crazy. Wait a minute: "Of course I love you Jesus, I talked in tongues 1978. I mean what do you want me to do? Get churchy? What are you trying to do? Turn us into a radical movement or something? I'll get excited about you when you come."

Who would want to drag us to Heaven? I mean...you're thinking Jesus is waiting for the Great Rapture Day when the church gets caught away, He's going to resurrect all the corpses, and all of a sudden on the way up we'll all get excited about seeing Him? ...Hadn't clapped, hadn't whistled, hadn't laughed, hadn't tried to win a soul for 30 years, but now that He's come; "You know I always was in love with you, I just wasn't boisterous and effervescent and vibrant and outgoing, I was a camouflage Christian, didn't want to offend nobody." I don't think you'd get three inches off the ground. Don't think so. Don't think so!

Just stay with me. "Behold I give you power", well, let me go back one. (18) "And he said unto them, I beheld Satan as lightening fall from heaven. (19) Behold, I give unto you power to tread on serpents and scorpions, and over all the power of the enemy: and nothing shall by any means hurt you. (20) Notwithstanding in this rejoice not, that the spirits are subject unto you; but rather rejoice, because your names are written in heaven." I'm still hung up on this thing about power encounters and it just really bothers me, because I don't know if we're really getting a hold of it. I talked to you about the apostolic church and the Book of Acts church and about trying to rescue the Book of Acts from being a history book, that it would be the living pattern to the New Testament church. And that, sometimes, God needs to upset our order, because some of our order may be disorder according to His concept, and we need for the Lord to help us understand about power encounters, because we are sent here to do one thing: rescue souls. And if I understand this Bible, Paul wrote to Timothy (2 Timothy 2:24-26) he says that we are trying to rescue people whom Satan takes at will and we are here to set captives free, and if Moses could not set two or three million Jewish captives free with just talk, we are insane to think that we are going to set people free, who are spiritually captive, by telling the devil, "Now you let him go." Let's do the one that we always do, "I command you in Jesus' name." "You let 'em go now." And if don't work, we yell louder as if He's deaf.

I don't think Jesus ever yelled at all. I don't. I don't think He'd ever say, "HEY!!!" No, I think He said, "Hey, get out of that guy." That devil just said, "Sure enough, yes sir." Sometimes he tore them and threw them on the ground, but he leaves. You never find any scripture of Jesus debating devils. He's never debating disease—"...Oh please go, come on, I've got my picture taken here, I've got some PR work, please leave, I've got my new Miracle magazine coming out now, would you please go?" That never happened. He just told leprosy, "Now get outta here." He told blindness and deafness, "You gotta go." There's never no debate. The debate comes with us. And the debate comes, because we're not sure what we're supposed to be doing. And I can tell right now that the sense of uncomfortableness is lifting up here.

What are we going to turn this church into? I hope something better then it is. Why should the government have to take care of all the drug heads and the drunks? I'll tell you why; because the church hasn't done its job. The church should be the most powerful entity on this planet. Well...well, well. The gospel is supposed to be declared and demonstrated. When Jesus started His ministry in Matthew 4 and Luke 4, the Bible said in Luke 4 that He went into the wilderness full of the Holy Ghost. The Bible says, about Verse 16, that when He came out of the wilderness, He came out in the power of the Holy Ghost. Well, did He have no power when He went in? No, the power is released when sin and evil is resisted. See, you can have the Holy Ghost and never have the power of the Holy Ghost, because the power is developed just like muscles are developed—from resistance. You have all the potential you need in your physical frame to develop bulges, biceps, and triceps. Oh yes you do. But you've got to fight against weights and you've got to strain your body and you've got to push it, and then when you push it, you tear your muscles down. That's what's called pumping iron.

When I used to pump iron, when I was younger, it was called; "boy, I've got a good burn there." A good burn meant you just tore a muscle. When you tore a muscle, the body has a chemical ability to send energy into those muscles and rebuild 'em, but when they rebuild 'em they get bigger. That's right. These guys you see walking around in these magazines...they've been tearin' and reparin' for the last three years. They just keep shredding muscles and chemistry just keeps rebuilding it bigger and bigger, and you look at those guys and you say, "How did you get like that?" Watch...; "I read a magazine." "I have a picture of Arnold Schwarzenegger in my bathroom." "I wrote Joe Widener a letter one year." All those kids, when we were growing up, we'd see those muscle-bound guys all with the oil on and all that, but we'd grab one of those... you could buy a pair of those squeeze things and you'd go at it, and you'd walk around and you'd squeeze it four or five times and you'd stop by a mirror and flex your muscles, intoxicated with your progress. The only thing that you had was that your wrist was hurting and your arm was hurting so bad you couldn't hardly make change. Am I telling the truth? Used to get those spring things...put 'em under your foot and just...and if they were too strong you unhook two of them and then you just finish 20 minutes and you walk in front of the mirror. "...We gotta get a bigger mirror here." "I need a carpenter to get these doors widened for me", and you'd made a muscle that looked like a pimple. But you felt like something had happened and the only guys that got bigger and more defined were the guys who went back to the workbench when they didn't want to. Hear me...when their muscles were aching and they were tired and there was nobody there to play the ram-jam box and there was nobody there to watch 'em and they just said, "No, I gotta go, it's time for my workout", and you watched these guys pumping iron and doing all this stuff and you say, "Man, that's crazy", but that's the difference between the guy who becomes successful and the guy who reads the magazine.

God deliver us from being a church that reads the magazine; and we don't get back to the workbench and get back to pumping the iron. How do you pump iron? You get in the prayer room. If this place is inconvenient, you make yourself a prayer room at your house, or in your car, or in your truck, and you interact with God. Why? Because as you break down, you build back up; as you get wounded, you get healed; as you invest in the power of prayer, God invests Himself and gives back to you an anointing of the Holy Ghost. And all of a sudden you wake up one day and you've got some authority. That's how it works! Don't misunderstand me, I hate that I always have to qualify stuff, but look; when I make a reference to me, I'm not blowing smoke about me, I'm just telling you because I'm allowed to travel a lot of places, I speak at Bible schools, I talk at different places and I've always got these young preacher kids asking me, you know, "How do you learn?" "How do you study?" "What are your study habits?" "How do you preach like you preach?" "How do you get like that?" "What do you do?" What they're asking is what we're always asking; "Could you give me 20 years in a shortcut?" "Could I have all that Heaven and no Hell?" "Could I have your success and your 12 best messages and forget about the 35,000 flops?"

I'm gonna go back to what I said years ago to this church; if you want my anointing, you better kill my lion. Hello, Samson. You want my anointing? Kill my lion. You want my crown? Kill my Goliath. You want to preach like me? Cry like me. Suffer like me. Feel loneliness and rejection like me. Know what it is to live with frustration and emptiness and sometimes even wrong concepts and ideas. If you want authority and you want power and you want to be able...then you've got to take the whole package. You can't just take a picture of some guy and preach it, or some lady, or some fella singin', or somebody playin' something; you gotta go through the dark nights, the lonely times when there's no applause, when people aren't there to say, "Whoa, you've done a wonderful job!" No, you gotta go through times when you've done the best and you feel frustrated and nobody says a kind word to you, and you walk out and you go home. What do you do? You go back in the prayer room, you bring it before God again, you try one more time. You ask God to help you again. Why? Because anointing isn't just given, anointing comes from crushing, the anointing oil comes from the breaking of the olives, it has to be crushed. If you want perfume, you gotta crush the petals of the flower. If you want bread, you gotta crush the corn. If God wants saints, He's gotta crush the saints.

I'm gonna tell you something, folks; the only thing that's gonna help us do what God wants us to do, is the anointing. And I'm here to tell you, unless I'm out of my mind, the anointing ain't free. The first dose you got is when you repented and sought God with all you heart, and God anointed you with the Holy Ghost, but I'm here to tell you; that anointing will not last more then a week or two. Now, I know I got people sittin' here thinkin' this lasts for 30 years. It ain't lasting for 30 years! The only reason some of you are here is 'cause you don't want to go to Hell. It ain't because your anointing is there. Be honest with me now. Is there anybody here besides me that knows that when you sit next to certain people or you talk to certain people or you ask certain people to pray for you, you sense an anointing? More so than in other people? It doesn't mean the other people don't love God and they're not saved, but there's something about an overflow anointing that comes out of people. It's because they learn how to pray, and they hunger for the things of God.

If I could give you any kind of gift, I would ask God to make all of us so desperately hungry for His presence. Not for His stuff, for Him. Remember the Master's hands are always crowded, because that's where the fishes and the loaves come, and that's where He heals the sick, but you know what? The lady with the issue of blood...she found it plenty open around His feet, because there's very few people around His feet, but there's a lot of virtue that flows out of the bottom of His robe. There's something precious that comes down. That's why He told us in the prophet Isaiah, "Unto this man will I look unto, my direction is toward him or her who's of a contrite and a broken spirit." He said; ...I dwell not only in the high and the lofty place of Heaven, but I got 2 zip codes; I live there and I dwell with the contrite, and the humble, and the broken of spirit.... That means that God lives that high that nobody can get to Him...if I humble myself and apologize and repent and admit that I'm not what I need to be and I wanna be better, God will condescend from that high and lofty place and come down right where I am and do business with me. That's what He said. Anybody besides me feel like you ought to have more power and more authority and more anointing, and kinda either angry, frustrated, or wanna know what it is that you ain't got it? Thank you, you're the people I'm talking to. The rest of you just keep playing church.

Now, I'm gonna tell you something: in two years Harry Potter's worshipers went from six thousand to 20 million last month. Now they say it's just reading, and, fine, you can read into anything you want. You can stretch things and make it—behind every bush is a devil.... I understand that, but I'm telling you; the principal of the book and the movies and the films and the stuff—is witchcraft. That's what it is. And the kids are just enamored with it, because they are being taught how to cast spells and be able to hurt people and do all kinds of stuff. Now, whether they ever tap into it, I don't know, but I'm thinking in 2 years from six thousand to 20 million? I'm not damning a one of these people, I just want to use it as an illustration—the hunger for the supernatural is here. It's here! Don't damn and condemn those people, because they're trying to step into something; they think the witch-world is real. Oh yeah, the spirit world is real! The problem is; God has decided what the entrance is and what the entrance ain't. And if anything gets into the spirit world and circumvents Jesus' name baptism, the Holy Ghost, the blood of the Lamb, and Jesus Christ, the Way, the Truth, the Door, the Light.... That is displeasing to God. And you get yourself into a lot of trouble dealing with a bunch of devils, I've told you that a hundred times. You can invite a devil in on an Ouija board, but you can't make it leave. Once you invite that dirtbag in, buddy, you've invited him.

Look, the Earth was given to mankind on a lease. Now, I realize it's not taught in Pentecost, but it is, anyway. We have a lease on this. God gave the Earth to mankind. Under the auspices of the sovereignty of God. Now God has never lost His sovereignty to the devil, the Earth is still the Lord's. When the Lord gave the Earth to mankind to be a vice ruler and a vice regent, it was under the divine sovereignty of God. God didn't take His sovereignty off and give it to that shmoe, Adam. He's never gonna do that. And He's never gonna deliver His sovereignty to the church, but He is going to give divine rulership and authority under the auspices of sovereignty. So He gave the Earth into the hands of man. That's Bible. Genesis

1:28; He gave man total dominion over this planet. Over the vegetable kingdom, the mineral kingdom, the animal kingdom, the foul of the air, the fish in the sea, He gave him dominion over it. When Adam...now watch; when Adam committed high treason and trespass, He took the dominion and gave it to Lucifer, and he became what the Bible says is: the god of this world. Small G (god). And when he tempts the lord in the wilderness and he flashes all these kingdoms in front of Jesus, he said here, watch, "If you'll fall down and worship me...", that's always the key—worship; "If you'll fall down and worship me, I'll give you these kingdoms and all their splendor, riches, and glory...", watch; "...for they have been delivered into my hand and I can give them to anybody I want." Why? "Because I'm now the god of this world."

Anybody besides me ever rented an apartment or a house? What's the name of the person that owns the joint? The landlord. But as long as you pay the lease, that landlord can't come in and use your bathroom and take a shower, or use your sink, or cook in you kitchen. That landlord can't just walk in one night while you're watching television and say;

"I want to watch Jackie Gleason, now turn on channel 7."

"What are you doing, you shmoe?"

"Well, this is my place."

Well, it's not your place as long as I have a lease. Is my rent current?"

"Yes."

"Then you ain't allowed in here."

Watch: Unless I, the tenant, invite you...now, I don't want to ruin your theology, but I'm gonna tell you what, he's the landlord, you're the tenants. He ain't allowed into your situation unless you invite him. That's the purpose of prayer. That's the purpose of prophetic prayer. That's why, when you get to prayin' in the spirit, do you know what you're actually doing? You're praying the mind and the will of God into a situation. That's why it's good to get anointed in prayer and talk in tongues and get into a prophetic utterance and an intercession of the Spirit, because then the Spirit prays through you and declares, in this Tera firma, His purpose and pleasure, and you give Him the release to do it. Don't you get it? When the prophets used to prophecy, do you know what they were doing? They were doing an utterance of the mind and will of God. "...Thus saith the Lord." "Hear ye the word of the Lord." It was an utterance of the mindset of God, because God needs permission. Why? He gave the planet to Adam. Adam gave it to Lucifer. He's the landlord, we're the tenants.

Watch; anybody besides me ever transferred a lease? Nope? Never did? Nobody? Well, let me give you a legal lesson. If I'm a tenant and you're the landlord, I can't, under our lease agreement, transfer my lease to another person even if they pay the money. You do the same thing if you transfer a debt and a lien on a car. You transfer it, if the document allows it. Earth's document allowed it. Adam had the lease. In trespass, he transferred it to Lucifer. Now he's the tenant. Guess what? He ain't inviting Him, so the slaves, the prisoners, and the hostage...God made a way. He gave you a gift called prayer, so if the hostage would pray, if the one that was cast out would pray, we can be inviting God back into the lease, and the landlord can step...well, I'll go a little further for you: Once Jesus got here and whipped the devil in the wilderness, and beat him up real bad at Calvary, and wiped him completely out at the resurrection...guess what? We're the tenants again, He's the landlord, and now we can invite Him into every situation we need, if we'll just pray.

So now watch; this is what made His ministry so powerful. You see, when Jesus showed up, He was the landlord wrapped up in some rags. And the devil said; "Oh I know who you are. Now that silly bunch of Israelites, they can't figure out who you are, but I know who you are; you're my ex-boss. You're the one who threw me out. I know who you are. You ain't got no business doin' stuff here."

Jesus could reply, "Oh, yeah? I commanded that lady's womb there. The womb of the woman is the door of life, I'm here legally, I got the camouflage rags on, but you watch me."

You know what all them devils were sayin'? "The landlord's here." "...the earth is the Lord's and the fullness thereof." The landlord's here. He's on an inspection tour. And, so, when He went to Calvary, He bought back the lease and He handed it back to the human race. He said; "Come on, let's start over. You can recover everything you lost from the first Adam. You can get back everything you lost from his mistake, because I'm here on a recovery mission. All you got to do is fast and pray and believe Me and call on My name and use My Word and I will operate according to the lease."

Did you get it? It's powerful stuff. So now God turns around and says, "Here, I have negated the other lease, I have restored it back to you." Now here's the problem; when God threw that other cat out of the lease, he's got an attitude. He wants back in the house. He wants to keep dictating how you live. He wants to mess with your thoughts. Oh, he wants to hold up that "G" word: Guilt. Shame, condemnation; pass, fail. Some of you folks are being held hostage by two things: your past and your future. Let me help you with it. I hate to give it away tonight, but I will, here it is: Your past is in the tomb and your future is in the womb. So all you got right now is the present, but the present is enough. Don't be held hostage by something that's been buried. Don't be held hostage by something that may never be born. Take care of this moment. Let this moment be your miracle. You can't do nothin' about tomorrow, and you sure can't do nothin' about yesterday, so why don't you use the miracle of this moment? Rewrite your story.

So, the whole issue was: when Jesus came walking here as the landlord, He started this thing...the New Testament Power Encounters. One power was going to encounter another. The Kingdom of God against the kingdom of Satan. The Kingdom of Light, the kingdom of darkness; Kingdom of Truth, kingdom of error; Kingdom of Life, kingdom of death. It's confrontation, and all four books of the Gospel shows nothing but daily and nightly confrontation. Confrontation! I mean, Jesus, as far as I can find, never had a peaceful day. I mean, He'd just try to go from over here to over there, and no matter what happens, the devil gets in His way. And He ain't looking for 'em! He says, "I must needs go down to Samaria." And getting down to Samaria, He finds this girl shackin' up with this guy and says, "I gotta deal with this now." Sets her free and forgives her of the mistakes she's made. My God, she's a better evangelist without the Holy Ghost then those of us with the Holy Ghost. She ain't got the Holy Ghost...she has one meeting with Jesus...brings the whole city out. "Come meet a man who told me everything ever I did, ain't that the Christ? Ain't that the Messiah?" We get the Holy

Ghost, talking in tongues and we go to work like.... See, our problem...I was taught this way coming up and it's wrong, I was taught that way and it's wrong...it wasn't intentional, but it came across unconsciously: Debate everybody—everybody that ain't lookin' like you, dressin' like you, talkin' like you, livin' like you, believe like you...they're all devils, they need help, debate 'em. I don't think so!

Hate sin? Yes. Love the sinner? Well...yeah, okay.... Don't you get it? We're on a scoundrel hunt. You shouldn't have to go far to find some. You could look in your own family. You could fill the choir with your family. Our deal is that we just don't want to offend nobody. Now, I understand that the Bible says, "He that winneth souls is wise." So does that also mean the opposite? "He that doesn't win souls is stupid"? What's the opposite of wise? Ignorant? Stupid? Have you ever thought about it? Two thirds of the word God is "go." The whole Great Commission is "go." When did we come up with "stay" and "sit"?

"Go ye into all the world, and preach the gospel to every creature." (Mark 16:15)

Go forth.

Tell everybody.

Go heal the sick.

CHAPTER FOUR
And when he came to his disciples, he saw a great multitude

Mark 9:14, "And when he came to his disciples, he saw a great multitude about them, and the scribes questioning with them." Now that's a sermon all by itself, because that's all scribes do is question. Scribes are Bible recorders. They were the people God used to write scripture. They are the self-appointed interpreters of scripture. You will never find a scribe praying for the sick. He just asks questions; he just makes sure you got it right according to his perception, but he won't heal the sick and he won't cast out a devil. He won't give a dime to somebody that's hungry. You don't want to be a scribe.

(15) "And straightway all the people, when they beheld him, were greatly amazed, and running to him saluted him. (16) And he asked the scribes, What question ye with them? (17)And one of the multitude answered and said, Master, I have brought unto thee my son, which hath a dumb spirit; (18) And wheresoever he taketh him, he teareth him: and he foameth, and gnasheth with his teeth, and pineth away: and I spake to thy disciples that they should cast him out; and they could not. (19) He answereth him, and saith,..." now I like this, he didn't say beans to his disciples. It says, "He answereth him." What? The guy that had the smirk on his face who said, "Your disciples couldn't get him cast out. Ha-ha. We brought him to your disciples, but your disciples couldn't cast him out. He-ha-he-ha."

(19) "He answereth him...," the smirky guy, "...O faithless generation, how long shall I be with you? how long shall I

suffer you? bring him unto me. (20) And they brought him unto him: and when he saw him, straightway the spirit tare him; and he fell on the ground, and wallowed foaming. (21) And he asked his father, How long is it ago since this came unto him? And he said, Of a child. (22) And ofttimes it hath cast him into the fire, and into the waters, to destroy him: but if thou canst do any thing, have compassion on us, and help us. (23) Jesus said unto him, If thou canst believe, all things are possible to him that believeth. (24) And straightway the father of the child cried out, and said with tears, Lord, I believe; help thou mine unbelief. (25) When Jesus saw that the people came running together, he rebuked the foul spirit, saying unto him, Thou dumb and deaf spirit, I charge thee, come out of him, and enter no more into him. (26) And the spirit cried, and rent him sore, and came out of him: and he was as one dead; insomuch that many said, He is dead. (27) But Jesus took him by the hand, and lifted him up; and he arose. (28) And when he was come into the house, his disciples asked him privately, Why could not we cast him out? (29) And he said unto them, This kind can come forth by nothing, but by prayer and fasting."

In Matthew 17:20 it reads, "...Because of you unbelief." You must get that. "...Because of your unbelief." Not because it wasn't my will to use you. It was because the level of your faith was lower than the level of your unbelief. It's almost as if Jesus looked at them and said, "Good try boys, come on, we'll do better next time."

Mark 16:14, "Afterward he appeared unto the eleven as they sat at meat...," see that's where you get the Pentecostal lifestyle, "they sat at meat." "...and upbraided them with their unbelief and hardness of heart, because they believed not them which had seen him after he was risen. (15) And he said unto them...," the ones that He had just rebuked and chided for unbelief, He says, "...Go ye into all the world, and preach the gospel to every creature." These are the folks He just chewed out for unbelief. He's now committing to them the destiny of every human soul according to the message they preach—these folks who were just chewed out for unbelief. It's kinda' like the Lord said, "Well I'm stuck with ya, you're all I got." No, you gotta hear me. You oughta' smile in your soul right now to be sayin' that;

"I'm stuck with us, too. But, but I can use ya'...I'm gonna' help you. I'm going to take you to a level of faith and confidence and trust. You're gonna become a mighty army. I can use you." Don't be held hostage because yesterday you flopped. These guys didn't even believe their own people that saw Jesus alive. He chewed 'em out for unbelief and said, "Okay, now let's go." He doesn't hold you hostage because you failed yesterday. He doesn't disenfranchise us from the work and dismiss and disconnect us from the source of energy because we failed. "We prayed for this person, it didn't work." Fine. Pray for the next one. He never says to you, "Well, you tried this before and you failed, why try it again?" He didn't say that. He says to these people, "Alright, go into all the world and preach the gospel to every creature." That's powerful.

He said in Mark 16:15, "Go ye into all the world, and preach the gospel to every creature. (16) He that believeth and is baptized shall be saved; but he that believeth not shall be damned. (17) And these signs shall follow them that believe; In my name shall they cast out devils; they shall speak with new tongues; (18) They shall take up serpents; and if they drink any deadly thing, it shall not hurt them; they shall lay hands on the sick, and they shall recover. (19) So then after the Lord had spoken unto them, he was received up into heaven, and sat on the right hand of God. (20) And they went forth, and preached every where...," like He commanded them, "...the Lord working with them, and confirming the word with signs following."

I'm back on my subject again: The Purpose and the Reason Of Power Encounters.

We have to grab a hold of the need for power encounters. It is the only thing that will turn a world away from Satan. You cannot talk people out of drug addiction. You cannot talk people out of drink. You cannot talk people and lecture people out of lust, and greed, and dishonesty, and villainy. It will not work. Most people that are doing vile and wicked things don't need a lecture; their conscience already tells em', "I'm not doin' right." But conscience itself is not enough to keep you and I from doing wrong. We need the power of God to help us. Even with the baptism of the Holy Ghost, there's a bunch of us, since we've been saved, have still done stupid things and dumb things and things we know we shouldn't have done. So the power of God was there, our conscience was working, the blood was there, but the human will has got a tremendous power to override all of that.

Remember when I told what the early apostolic church was? It was not a movement, it was not an organization; it was a walking incarnation of spiritual energy. I can't get away from that statement. I keep writing it down over and over again. The early church was an incarnation, a walking incarnation of divine energy; so much energy that the world was afraid of the church. Yeah, I got a whole lesson on that, that I haven't taught yet. In the early days, people were afraid to join themselves to the church, because God would show up and kill folks. God would use gifts of the Spirit and expose people's shenanigans. You read it; there's a lot of scripture that says, "...and great fear came upon the people, and they did not join themselves to the apostles or the church, for they were afraid." Because the early church was so committed to Jesus Christ and holy living, that unholy whoremongers, fakers and hypocrites would not dare come in among these sanctified ones and sit there and bring there vile trash in as if the church was nothing more than another organization.

Things have really changed. Things have really changed. There was a time when people wouldn't even curse in front of a church house. They'd take their hat off in front of women. They'd put a cigarette in their hand and cup it. Now they bring em' in their pocket and smoke in the bathroom! Now they come in and chase our girls and pursue them like a bunch of predators. We need the power of God to become stronger in our lives. Now, I didn't say to be judgmental towards people. No, we're not the judge. God's the judge. If we can get to a level of power in the Spirit, that we live and move in the Spirit, there will be an awe about the Kingdom of God that will stun people. The Bible...that's what Psalm 1 is: that the ungodly and the sinner cannot stand in the way of the righteous and the holy. They don't come in and do that...folks it'd be terrifying. If you knew that in every service when you came together, God would be standing here, and God would inspect people's motives and desires, man, would we be prayerful people.

I'm just gonna go slow here. In Acts Chapter 3, Verse 6, we know what happened. Peter and John going up to the temple to pray, going past the man at the Gate Beautiful, there's some kinda quickening in his spirit...he senses either a gift of the Spirit, or a voice of God, or something. And he says, "Silver and gold have I none, but such as I have I give thee: In the name of Jesus Christ of Nazareth rise up and walk." The man leaps up and jumps, his ankle bones receive strength, he jumps up and down, he's worshipping God, he's running all over the place. From that miracle, God used that to create a platform so that 4,000 people were swept into the Kingdom. So the miracle of healing and deliverance is not an end in it self; it is a means to an end. It's always a means to an end.

So in Chapter 4 we read, (1) "And as they spake unto the people, the priests, and the captain of the temple, and the Sadducees, came upon them, (2) Being grieved that they taught the people, and preached through Jesus the resurrection from the dead." Now that's interesting that it would mention the priest, the captain of the temple, and the Sadducees, because the Sadducees were the people who were anti-supernatural-anything. They are with us today in Pentecost. "Having a form of godliness, but denying the power thereof:" (2 Timothy 3:12). Sadducees denied the resurrection, they denied the spirit world, and they denied angels or any interactions with angels. That's Bible. That's why Jesus told the people; ...look, you wanna beware the doctrine of the Pharisees, watch out for the leaven of Herod, and watch out for the doctrine of leaven of the Sadducees.

There's three things He warned us to watch out for: The Pharisee is the play actor—it's the hypocrite. You gotta watch out for the leaven of the Pharisee—it's the kingdom of "I'm really not what you think I am" ...the law person without mercy, watch out for that doctrine. Then He said watch out for the leaven of Herod—Herod is the doctrine that says, "I'm king, and if you endanger me, I will kill you, don't ever try to take me off my throne." That's why Herod killed all those Jewish babies, because he heard another king was born in Bethlehem, so he killed everything from two years down. That's the doctrine of Herod. But the doctrine of the Sadducees is scary, because the Sadducees were religious people. They were in-depth scripture studiers, but they did not believe in the supernatural. They denied the resurrection.

Remember the story in Acts, when Paul is being tried? He comes from Felix Festus and he's going to Agrippa. The Bible says when he's in this thing and one yells one thing and one yells another, and the Bible says Paul perceived that one group was Sadducee and one was Pharisee. He turned around and said...he just jumped up and said, "The question of the resurrection, that's what I'm being called into." All of a sudden the Pharisees jumped up and said, "What?" And they said, "Oh, if the man has seen an angel or a spirit has talked to him, we find no fault with him." So he played the two ends against the middle and got himself out of that fix, because he knew the Sadducees didn't believe in spiritual things.

Now, what I never understood about the Sadducees is, why would you go to church, anyway? If you don't believe in supernatural wonderment and visitations of God's Spirit and supernatural power to change your life or assist you in your times of trial and testing and sorrow and pain, why not go to an Amway meeting, instead? At least you could sell some soap and make some money. Why not go to a Shackly meeting, or why not join the Moose Lodge? Why not march in a parade and build a hospital for the Shriners? At least they're doin' some good for their fellow man. Why not go to a church that is on record as saying, "Now we don't want none of that supernatural junk around here. You jump up and talk in tongues around here, we'll throw your keister right out in the street, buddy. We don't believe in none of that gift stuff here"? The silence here is one of two things: the Sadducees are here, or I've just stunned you with truth.

Acts 4:3, "And they laid hands on them, and put them in hold unto the next day: for it was now eventide. (4) Howbeit many of them which heard the word believed; and the number of the men was about five thousand. (5) And it came to pass on the morrow, that their rulers, and elders, and scribes...," they got ready to bring him out. They brought him out and they started asking the question: "We wanna know by what power or by what name you've done this?

So Peter stands up full of the Holy Ghost and says, "By the name of Jesus this man is made whole." Now you have to understand what he was saying. He wasn't saying like we Pentecostals think, that the name of Jesus is a rabbit's foot that you rub, or a magic talisman, Open says me." That's what we do a lot, "...in the name of Jesus." It doesn't work a lot of times, because that's not what he was doing. What he was saying, "...in the name of Jesus," he was saying, "Oh, ya know the guy you murdered? God raised Him up, He's ascended to Heaven, He's alive, and He's messin' with ya." That's what he was meaning by "...in the name of Jesus", because the name of a dead man wouldn't help nobody. But he was insinuating that the dead man wasn't dead, that this Jesus was alive, because he goes on in the next few verses and said, "You killed Him, hung Him on a tree, threw Him in a ditch, but God raised Him up and made Him to be Lord and Christ to this world, and He's King of Kings and He's Lord of Lords." What he's trying to say is, "You know that Jesus who walked around with you and He was healing the sick and cleansing the lepers, and raising the dead and casting out devils? He's alive, and now He's using us guys."

See, the problem that the Sadducees, the scribes, and the Sanhedrin were having was; first, they didn't believe in Jesus; secondly, they refused to believe He was alive; third, they were absolutely crazy, because these unlearned and ignorant men had been used by God to heal a man.

In the next three verses they turn around, put him aside, and say, "Now, what are we gonna do about this?" Read it, it says, (16) "For that indeed a notable miracle hath been done by them...and we cannot deny it", ...now we can call them liars, but this idiot up here keeps jumpin' up and down and runnin' all over the place and we watched him for forty years sittin' at the gate....

Well, let me try it again. See this young lady right over here who's been running all over the building? Now you say anything you want to, but you can't deny that her foot went straight. She stood up, she's runnin' around, she's still walkin' and she's not walkin' on her walker.... My God, there oughta be a jubilee in our hearts that says, "You wanna see a miracle? We got one sittin' right here!"

Now, what was the whole issue? Let me get back to it. A power encounter: The power of crippling disease and ailment that this poor man had before he was even born. He was born crippled. Something happened, probably during mama's pregnancy, where something didn't develop right, some kind of body chemistry didn't work, an organ wasn't developed, a bone didn't move, or marrow didn't come. Something didn't happen, so that when the child was born, the child couldn't stand up and it never did stand up. For 40 years it never learned to walk, and then in one moment the name of Jesus and the power of another world says, "Walk", and he just...BOOM...gets up.

Now you know a child has to learn how to walk. This is a phenomenal miracle. Jesus didn't go, "Well, practice awhile." No, He turned around and said, "Up and at em' boy!" The Bible says, (Acts 3:7) "...immediately his feet and ankle bones received strength, and he walking and leaping...." I mean, God overran six to ten months of baby stuff...tryin' to learn how to walk in one minute. See, God can get you and I to do stuff that would take us years to do. God can do it in just a moment, if we can have a power encounter.

So they go through this thing, (Acts 4:11) "This stone which was rejected by the builders, which is become the head of the corner. (12) Neither is there salvation in any other: for there is none other name under heaven given among men, whereby we must be saved." Now I like the way Peter put that in, because he's a soul winner. They've asked him, "How did you do this miracle?" He touches the miracle and then just kinda takes a fast turn around second base and says, "Let's talk about salvation." Ain't nobody asked about salvation. Ain't none of them Jews wanna know about salvation. They wanna know how the crippled guy is jumpin' up and down and runnin' around. He said, "By the name of Jesus, the one that you killed that God raised, He's on high, He's working through us now. Now listen, you boys need to be saved." They get furious at him. The Bible said they want to kill him, because he said, (Verse 12) "Neither is there salvation in any other: for there is none other name under heaven given among men, whereby we must be saved."

So what happens? The next verse (13) "...and they took knowledge of them, that they had been with Jesus." I prayed that this morning, that somehow God would help my life, that I could somehow impact people that I meet, so that they could say, not that I'm a smart guy, or I'm a good preacher or something, but, "Man, that guy's been with Jesus." Boy, that was weak. I thought you'd a been on your feet, talking in tongues or running the aisles just then. I thought for sure your heart woulda jumped up and said,

"Yeah, that's what I want." Some of you I think say all you want is for people to say, "They've been to the bank and made another deposit...."

The Bible says that when they said that, they took counsel to slay them, but they didn't know what to do with them. The whole issue came out of a power encounter. I want you to get this. They threatened them; they said;

"Don't talk in His name, don't teach in His name."

Peter says, "Well, what's right in the sight of God? You have to decide. We're only doing what God told us."

He's not being disrespectful. See, if you have a Sergeant that tells you to do something and you have a General that tells you do something, forget the Sergeant. Am I right? Sorry, I don't care, the Sarge just got out-ranked. The Sarge says, "I want you to go over there and pick up them papers." Then General walks up and says, "What are you doing pickin' up them papers?"

"Well the first Sarge said I need to pick em' up."

"I told you to get over there and fix that car."

"Yes sir!"

Well, the Sanhedrin says, "We want you to stop preaching in the name", but the Captain of our salvation said, "Preach on, boys."

Now, you ain't gotta worry, because He's going to back us up if we do what He tells us to do. Sometimes, when we do what He tells us to do, it's going to cause a conflict and a clash with the powers that be. That's just part of the geography. So, when something comes against you and you've done the will of God, don't fuss and cuss with it, just turn around and say, "Talk to the Captain." The Bible says that they go back to their people.

Am I boring you? I know it'd be very rude if you said, "Yes", just...they go back to their crew and they tell them all that has happened to them. How they "threatened us, they're gonna whip us up and do all kinds of mean stuff with us," and they get a big kick out of it. They go to prayin'. Here's the thing, in Verse 29 he says, "And now, Lord, behold their threatenings: and grant unto thy servants, that with all boldness they may speak thy word." They did not say...which I have read into this for 20 years...and I just saw it, they did not say, "Give us boldness to preach." They didn't say that. They said, "Give us boldness to speak your word." Why did he say that? Because everybody in the body was supposed to speak the word. I've read this for 20 years thinking that Peter, because he's a Pentecost preacher, that he's asking God to give him anointing, strength and boldness to preach the word. That's not what he said. He said, "Grant thy servants boldness that they may speak thy word." Speak. Not yell. Speak. Not scream. Speak.

How are we going to get boldness? Verse 30, "By stretching forth thine hand to heal; and that signs and wonders may be done by the name of thy holy child Jesus. (31) And when they had prayed, the place was shaken where they were assembled together; and they were all filled with the Holy Ghost, and they spake the word of God with boldness." Watch: and God gave great witness to His Word by backing up what they were saying, because He said, "these signs shall follow them that believe." Then in Mark 16:20 it says, "And they went forth, and preached every where, the Lord working with them, and confirming the word with signs following." You need to make that a prayer every morning and every night in your life.

You need to start praying that. "God give us boldness to be your witnesses. Give us boldness, not brashness, rudeness, and unkind...give us boldness." Why? We are supposed to be testifiers. What do you do? You testify of what you've experienced, what you've heard, and what you've seen. You don't have to testify about everything you know about the Bible, just share with people what has happened to you, prayers that have been answered, or the goodness of God that's worked in your life. Folks don't need to be preached at and preached to, they just need to be told.

In Mark Chapter 5 when the Lord cast 2,000 devils out of a Gadarene streaker-man living in a cemetery, He didn't go do a dissertation on Daniel 11 and Daniel 9...Nebuchadnezzar's image...how much does the moon way...and just exactly how fast does light travel. He turned around and said, "Go tell your friends and your loved ones what the Lord's done for you and showed compassion on you." He didn't ask him to give him a dissertation. Tell people what's happened in you life, and if they are responsive and receptive, God is saying, "I will lead you what else to say and I'll confirm my word with signs." I think the reason that we're not getting more signs done in our daily life is because we don't give God enough time to do it. Our mission is still to rescue the lost. That's our mission—to represent Jesus Christ to this world.

Okay, Acts 5:12, "And by the hands of the apostles were many signs and wonders wrought among the people; (and they were all with one accord in Solomon's porch. (13) And of the rest durst no man join himself to them: but the people magnified them." See, people were afraid to join the early church. There was no such thing as Mr. Graham and the rest of the boys joinin' the church. That's not Bible. They were afraid to join themselves to the apostles and the apostolic church. Why? There was such a difference and distance between the apostolic church and the world around them. They weren't gonna get with those holy rollers unless they meant business, because they had seen the radical transformation take place in their lives.

We have a sanctifying influence of the Holy Ghost, but we have to make that power available in our lives by contrition, brokenness, consistent practice, and Bible study. It's not automatic. Because you received the Holy Ghost, I promise you, the Holy Ghost will not just automatically work in you and slap you in the head and all that stuff. Oh, the Holy Ghost will cause conviction, but you keep not feeding the spirit.... You feed the spirit with prayer. You feed the spirit...the spirit man...with the strength of the Word, with fellowship with godly people, with worship services, with prayer services, and with fasting. That's how you strengthen the spiritual man. You cannot get the Holy Ghost and expect the Holy Ghost to stay in your body...your spirit...for 20 years, and you do nothing for it. You can't be a threat to Hell that way; it's impossible. The natural man will get stronger all the time, 'cause the strongest drive you have is preservation, and the natural man is gonna make sure he don't get hurt.

Acts 5:14, "And believers were the more added to the Lord, multitudes both of men and women.) (15) Insomuch that they brought forth the sick into the streets, and laid them on beds and couches, that at the least the shadow of Peter passing by might overshadow some of them. (16) There came also a multitude out of the cities round about unto Jerusalem, bringing sick folks, and them which were vexed with unclean spirits: and they were healed every one." Did you get that? "...and they were healed every one." What is it saying? Jesus was still doing in them what He had done in Himself when He walked. He had not changed His purpose, He had not diminished in His power, and He had not in any way altered what He had been doing in His own body. I told you before, the church is supposed to be Jesus Christ's replacement body on the planet. We are God's second body of Christ. The first body of Christ was crucified, buried, resurrected, and ascended. We are the body of Christ. The same energy source and power that worked in Jesus of Nazareth is supposed to be working in us.

Well, it said that He healed them all. That was a power encounter; the power of God coming against the power of sickness, devils, diseases, and sin. Sin is a powerful force in the world. It's taken millions of people to a devil's Hell. You cannot talk people out of sin. We've got a world of so-called Christian churches; they're trying to *reform* people out of sin. You can't do that. People have to be *born* out of one kingdom into another kingdom, and that takes the baptism of the Holy Ghost. *Power Encounter.*

Acts 8:5, "Then Philip went down to the city of Samaria, and preached Christ unto them. (6) And the people with one accord gave heed unto those things which Philip spake, hearing and seeing the miracles which he did. (7) For unclean spirits, crying with loud voice, came out of many that were possessed with them: and many taken with palsies, and that were lame, were healed. (8) And there was great joy in that city." Then it talks about a sorcerer named Simon, the sorcerer who had bewitched the city. They said he was the great power of God...showing you how stupid the human spirit is: It can't tell the difference between the devil working and God working. The guy bewitched it with sorceries. Read the scriptures, he bewitched them. It's in Verse 9, "But there was a certain man, called Simon, which beforetime in the same city used

sorcery, and bewitched the people of Samaria, giving out that himself was some great one:
10) To whom they all gave heed, from the least to the greatest, saying, This man is the great power of God." You must be kidding! Because they don't understand the source of the supernatural, they think the supernatural is God. That's why you have all these loonies with Ojai boards, witchcraft, and all this foolishness. Watch; he had bewitched them a long time with his sorceries. Verse 12, "But when they believed Philip preaching the things concerning the Kingdom of God, and the name of Jesus Christ,..." you gotta get that, every time the Kingdom of God is preached, miracles, signs and wonders are supposed to happen.

Jesus was the representation of the Kingdom of God. He came with a power source to challenge all the evil. According to 1 John 3:8 he said, "...For this purpose was the Son of God manifested, that he might destroy the works of the devil." Now, if we are in sync with Jesus, we are His children and His body, and we have His name and His Spirit, would you please tell me what we're supposed to be doing? Please don't insult me by saying we're supposed to be doing something different. Jesus came healing all that were oppressed of the devil, for God was with Him. He came to destroy the works of the devil. Now we've been left to finish His work.

Now, what are we supposed to be doing? We cannot give our lives to maintain a building or maintain our heritage. That's not what we're here for. We are here to take captives out of Satan's kingdom, loose bound people, give people a chance to make a decision, find demon-possessed people and cast devils out of them, so that people have a right to make a decision. If they choose to go to Hell, God will let them go to Hell, but He wants them to have a choice. It's not fair for hundreds of millions of people to be damned to a devil's Hell, because they've been hoodwinked and fooled by the god of this world and the mind-blinder had blinded their minds and they don't understand it. They're not wicked and evil people because they don't understand it. We've got to bring light to people. We've got to bring illumination to people, but it takes more than a lecture. It takes a power encounter. Remember, he went down and preached Christ unto them and the Kingdom of God, and then God backed it up with mighty signs, wonders, and miracles. So the people believed, because of what they heard and what they saw. Declare; demonstrate. Proclaim; perform.

Please hear me; two prayer requests for our church, get it in your craw: Acts 4:30, "By stretching forth thine hand to heal; and that signs and wonders may be done by the name of thy holy child Jesus." And; God, start confirming your Word in my life. That ain't gonna fill nobody with pride, because you know you couldn't heal nobody, you couldn't save nobody, you can't give nobody the Holy Ghost, and you can't forgive nobody's sins. So you need to start asking God every day, "Okay Lord, if I'm supposed to be the second replacement body of Christ, and I'm supposed to be the headquarters of this 'you working on this planet right now,' then I'm asking you to give me boldness to be a witness and declare what you've done in my life and share truth with people." "Grant me a sensitivity of the spirit." "Please confirm Your Word with signs following." A Power Encounter.

What happened? Why did the great revival take place in Samaria? They had a power encounter. The power of Jesus Christ that was incarnate in Phillip's spirit challenged the power of witchcraft and sorcery that was coming out of this sorcerer Simon. Remember, every kingdom has got its power and its representative. Evil's got a power coming from Satan; its representative was Simon. Here comes the Kingdom of God, trottin' down into Samaria, through this lowly guy Phillip the evangelist, and God's got His representative. So he walks in and *Boom*, power encounter, and all of a sudden the kingdom of Satan goes down. Why? Jesus is there. Don't you get it? The spirit that manipulated and moved and governed Simon recognized the Jesus in Philip, because Jesus had been there before in John Chapter 4 with the Samaritan woman. Spirits don't forget those things. They walk, they say, "Uh, oh, you were here before with that lady." "We know who you are," and it wilted. If you read the rest of this scripture, the Bible says that Simon, himself, was baptized.

I'm gonna go a little further, I'm gonna mess with theology. I'll show you from this scripture that Simon got the Holy Ghost. Most Pentecostals debate me and say it didn't happen. Oh yes it did. Read with me, Acts 8:13, "Then Simon himself believed also: and when he was baptized," Was he baptized? Come on, get strong; was he baptized? Was he baptized in Jesus name? Okay, now watch this, "...he continued with Philip, and wondered, beholding the miracles and signs which were done. (14) Now when the apostles which were at Jerusalem heard that Samaria had received the word of God," not the Spirit of God, but the Word of God, "...they sent unto them Peter and John: (15) Who, when they were come down, prayed for them," who is them? Them that was baptized. Watch: "...who, when they were come down, prayed for them, that they..." who's the *they*? It's the them, "...that they might receive the Holy Ghost: (16) (For as yet he was fallen upon none of them:" who was the *them*? Them is the *they*. Who's the *they*? They is *them*. Who is *them*? The guys baptized.

Let me try it again. Jerusalem heard that Samaria had received the Word. They hadn't received the Holy Ghost; they'd received the Word, so they sent Peter and John to pray for them who were baptized. Was Simon baptized? Here ya go, (17) "Then laid they..." the apostles "...their hands on them,"...who's the *them*? The *baptized*. "...and they..." who's the *they*? It's the *them*. Who's the *them*? The *baptized*. "...received the Holy Ghost." Now we'd like to do this pretty little Pentecostal protocol thing and say that the apostles came down and prayed for all them that were baptized, except Simon, because he was at lunch. Oh no! They prayed for *them* who were baptized and *them* received the Holy Ghost. Why, because the only thing you need to get the Holy Ghost is to repent and seek God and praise Him, and He'll give you the Holy Ghost.

Now I'm gonna go a little further. That's why you need more than the Holy Ghost, because every one of us, when we get the Holy Ghost, we still got a suitcase of baggage. We get all kinds of stuff that's unsettled. That doesn't mean we don't love God. Doesn't mean we're not saved. It means that we've got stuff that the Holy Ghost is gonna start pointing out to us and helping us, so that we can...what? Get conformed to the image of Jesus Christ. When you and I received the Holy Ghost and are baptized in Jesus' name, we're not conformed to the image of Jesus Christ; we just received a Spirit adoption and got into the Kingdom. Come on now, stop bein' so religious with me right now. As we walk along, God starts pointing to, pressing on pressure points, and pushing on stuff and saying;

"Hey, how 'bout this? Hey what about...? Well, this attitude needs a little help here. Well, ya got a little lust over here and there's some greed over here. You know, you lose your temper to easy and, ya know, you speak your mind too much."

"Well I got the Holy Ghost."

"Right, but the Holy Ghost is trying to get you."

See; real holiness is not hair piled high and a dress adhesive-taped to your ankles. Real holiness is a life that is full of light, having no dark part. See, I can't claim that, I got too many blotches and blemishes, but I am opening my spirit every day to God that He may deal with the weak areas of my life and bring me into conformity to His image. Yes, I wouldn't mind being a great Pentecostal. I'd much rather be a great Christian. I'd much rather be a person that's conformed to the image of God. I'd much rather have God just keep putting light on in side of my spirit, so that my outer action would match my inner anointing. As God finishes me, I want to be more like Him than when I first started.

If we are not getting more like Jesus; if we don't want to be in Jesus' presence; if we'd rather watch TV, take trips, work our job, and lay around and do stuff, rather than be in His presence, we are not becoming holy and we are not pursuing holiness. Holiness is not an *it*; holiness is the grandest thing that charges the entire atmosphere of Heaven. Everybody in Heaven and everything in Heaven is holy and nobody is unhappy. I'm here to tell ya; holiness is a positive thing. It's not a negative thing; it's a positive thing.

You know...you can be married...like some of you, or you can be happily married, like a few of us. I'm serious. Big difference. Just because you have a certificate, "I'm Married", that don't guarantee nothin' except you're allowed to go to bed and live in the same house. That's it. Other than that, you're going to have to work at it. You can't throw the certificate up and slap your wife in the face and say, "Hey, I'm married, get them pots rattlin' girl. I'm the king of this palace." You're gonna be a bachelor in that palace is what you're gonna be. You're gonna get a Posturepedic couch, so you get a good night's rest...is what your gonna get. You can't slap that woman in the face with your marriage certificate and demand of her some performance. Oh, come on ladies...and you can't slap him in the face with your certificate, 'cause then you ain't got a marriage, you got a legal agreement. Now just look straight ahead...you're sittin' next to your husband or wife acting like I never even reached you.

Did you get it? Excuse me, I was bein' deceptive, I know exactly where I was. I was just tryin' to break that heat that's comin' towards me. We know the rest of this verse, and this is what always scared me. Simon turns around and says to Peter, (Acts 8:18) "And when Simon saw that through laying on of the apostles' hands the Holy Ghost was given, he offered them money, (19) Saying, Give me also this power, that on whomsoever I lay hands, he may receive the Holy Ghost." Wait a minute, Simon's been baptized in Jesus' name and Simon has the Holy Ghost, but he's perverted. Watch; when you get the Holy Ghost, you bring with you; stuff. Guess what he brought with him? His previous manipulation over a city. All he was gonna do was transfer kingdoms and bring his prowess from that kingdom to this Kingdom and be a Pentecostal manipulator.

Do you know that we have people in this church, like at anybody else's church, who are very good at some things and very successful in certain areas, and they still get frustrated, because they try to bring their stuff from the world's kingdom into the church and think it oughta work the same. Nope. You can be a sharp man and make millions of dollars out there; God will require humility and brokenness in here. All of us do it. All of us do it! "Well, I was good there, I'm gonna do that here, I'll just sanctify it." Anybody ever heard of the great Pentecostal man called Marx? Anybody ever heard of the Communist Karl Marx? You ever heard about Karl Marx, who he was, how it happened, what took place? Interesting story—Karl Marx. Son of a Jewish man, moved from Germany to England, joined a denominal church—his father did. Because his father was a Jewish business man and his father said, "I'm gonna leave the synagogue and the temple and I'm gonna join this denominational church, because I can have many good business contacts there", he prostituted one-God truth for business contacts. Now watch, this is a true story. Karl Marx's writings tell the story. He says;

> "As a young man, a Jewish, one-God, Abraham-seed man, I became extremely disillusioned with my father's religion—how easily he prostituted his belief for business. I become disillusioned with the church we were in, for it was a sham."

So he left there and wrote the "Communist Manifesto", in which he wrote, "Religion is simply the Opiate of the people." That birthed the tirade called Communism, because a man said, "I'll take business from outside in the carnal world and I'll sanctify it and put it in a church service and I'll make money." God help us.

There's some stuff we just gotta leave outside when we step into the Kingdom. We gotta pull our shoes off and say, "Holy, holy, holy, is the Lord God Almighty." The Lord don't need our wisdom, He don't need our gold, He don't need our ability, and He don't need our prowess. He's all-wise, all-knowing, and all-powerful. He fills all time and space, He transcends time and space. He's in my tomorrow, He knows about my yesterday and He knows what I'm dealing with. He knows every fracture of my personality and He knows every weak-kneed effort in my life. I need Him; He doesn't need me. I make money, He makes gold. I move through time, He lives in eternity. My God in Heaven...we need the Lord to take our shoes off...walk into the Kingdom and the church and say, "Holy!" I'm talkin' about power encounter...power encounters. I talked to you about Moses at the bush. I talked to you about Moses with the magicians. I talked to you about Jacob and his wrestling match, but I'm tryin' to get a little further along on this journey.

Acts Chapter 9, Verse 5; We owe two-thirds of the written New Testament Bible to a man who was receptive to a power encounter. Apostle Paul on the road to Damascus...you talk about a man who has a power encounter. You know what scares me? Apparently he didn't have any power encounters with the church people he ran into. That scares me, because they were going everywhere healing the sick, casting out devils, and raisin' the dead, and all of a sudden, somehow, the group of people he meets he was so unimpressed with that he murdered, he slashed them, he made them blaspheme, he threw 'em in jail, and he hauled 'em everywhere. Something didn't come out of those people that spoke of Jesus. ...said "I better do this one myself." Now that's scary.

That makes me wonder, just where is my spiritual temperature? This guy arrested untold numbers of Christians, slaughtered them, damaged them, jailed them...city after city, and yet he never had a power encounter—except one. He had a brush with a power encounter when they crushed Stephen's head and they stoned him to death. They watched, for a moment a window open up; "Receive my spirit, lay not this sin to their charge," and then the window closed. I have to believe when Saul of Tarsus...because he held the garments of those that stoned Stephen...for a moment, the power of genuine mercy, compassion, and forgiveness grabbed him and shook him to his soul—for a moment. Then he just shook it off and he went back to just his tirade of hatred and making havoc of the church, until finally Jesus Christ Himself steps in and intercedes and interrupts in this man's life, and knocks him off beat and starts talkin' to him—I mean directly to him.

You say, "Boy, if I could only have a power encounter like that." You've had one if you got the Holy Ghost, because I wanna tell you something; you didn't get the third person of the trinity when you got the Holy Ghost, you God Jesus of Nazareth when you got the Holy Ghost. When you spoke in tongues, it was Jesus of Nazareth talking through you. Oh yeah, the Spirit speaketh, maketh utterance...just uses your human brainwork, but you got Jesus Christ in you, the hope of glory.

So Jesus just knocks him down and he gets a power encounter. What happened? Any time there's a power encounter...listen to me; energy is released, power is released. I told you that last week. That happens in the natural world. When hot air and cold air collide, when wind currents move, when all kinds of gravitational pulls work, and they align with planets and stars, there's a tremendous release of energy that takes place. When there's a power encounter in the earth, energy is released and you have a split in the earth, the plates move, and an earthquake takes place. Any time there's a power encounter, something happens, and power encounters can be very terrifying, because they have no perimeters in which it is safe and not safe. That's why when you have a hurricane and earthquake; man, it's dangerous, because you just don't' know what's gonna happen because it's this great power.

The wind that was in that hurricane that come up in North Carolina, leveled places, and ten miles away, just destroyed stuff, and eighty and ninety mile an hour winds...I heard the guy on the radio talking about bein' ten miles from the sea and a fifteen foot wave came and beat against his house for a half hour 'til his house just came to the ground. He said, "I think I'm movin'." He said, "It is the third hurricane I've been in and this time it took my house, and I think I'm outta here." I'm talkin' about power encounters.

The power encounter was what apostle Paul needed. He didn't need a lecture, and he didn't need the mealy-mouthed testimony of a bunch of half-backslidden apostolic people. He needed God to grab him and say, "Hey! You gotta problem with me?"

All of a sudden he said, "Who, who are you?"

"I'm Jesus, the one that you're killin' all these people over that you say that I'm not alive, but I am alive. What do you wanna do now?"

But see, the power encounter...you gotta understand something; Paul was not dishonest. That's why he became such a mighty vessel of God. He was mistaken, but he wasn't dishonest. He was wrong in his concept, his error of theology, but he was honest, because the minute the power encounter grabbed him, he turned around, apologized, and said, "I'm wrong. What do you want me to do?" See, that's the purpose of a power encounter; it's to bring us face-to-face with ourselves and see whether we're real or not.

When Nathan the prophet sticks his prophetic finger in the face of King David and said, "Thou art the man." You talk about a power encounter! Now, guess what this was? This was the test of the integrity of David: "We'll find out whether David wants to be real or not."

> "You're exposed. Took a man's wife to bed, you got her pregnant, you murdered her husband, and you played a hypocrite for a year. You're the man, next move is yours."

Now he could turn around and say, "Kill this guy."

David could say, "I don't know what you're talkin' about."

That happens; I see it happen here week in and week out. I watch the presence of God touch people and ya kinda go, "I don't know what he's talkin' about," and walk out when you shoulda come forward, hold on, and never move. The power encounter is showing dishonest—dishonest—dishonest—..."doesn't really want to know Me, very satisfied at the level of their present spiritual operation, don't wanna come close, might cost 'em commitment"...dishonest.

Anybody besides me ever had the presence of the Lord touch you. Wait a minute; touch you and maybe you start having tears or a lump in your throat, and you sense, without even thought; apology, confession. Before you're even premeditating anything, you're saying, "Oh God, I just...Lord I just need some help. I'm not what I oughta be. Jesus please help me." Anybody? Has that ever happened to anybody besides me? You know what that is? That's a power encounter that's checking the level of your integrity.

The colliding forces in a power encounter that produce energy and surges that become released are so difficult to control, so messy, scary, and disorderly, that most of us learn to stay away from them and avoid them. I'm gonna give you one more and then I'll stop: Acts Chapter 13, Verse 4, "So they, being sent forth by the Holy Ghost..."

Hold it, excuse me, finishing my last point about integrity...Mark Chapter 5, the Gadarene, cast out the devils, remember that? Now remember this man has tormented their neighborhood for untold days. He's terrified the whole area because they've gone out many times, tried to bind him with ropes and chains and couldn't bind him, so he was a problem to their community. Jesus comes out in one power encounter:

"Come out of the man!"

"Let us go in the pigs."

"Go!"

Go in the pigs? They experienced a power encounter that would alter their lifestyles and they'd rather have the pigs than the demon possessed man, so they asked Jesus to leave. See what a power encounter does? It'll make you reveal your real colors. Killed their pigs? Yeah, but You saved a man. This man may become the Mayor of the city. He might be the greatest benefactor you ever have. He may be a blessing to his family and his children. He might become a great surgeon or a doctor or something. "What are You doing, our pigs, our money, our way of life?" Watch what they...power encounters will make you do stupid things. They turned around and asked the source of divine relief, "Leave us alone." "Go away." "Don't hang around here." "We don't like this unpredictable stuff."

"You might start talkin' about stuff we're doin'." They asked the only One that could fix them, to leave.

That's dumber than the one that's second in line...when Saul throws javelins at David; the idiot is trying to kill the only giant killer Israel has. Ain't nobody in the whole nation can kill a giant but David, and this nut is trying to kill him. That's like you and I trying to kill each other.

One more verse. (Acts 13:4) "So they, being sent forth by the Holy Ghost, departed unto Seleucia; and from thence they sailed to Cyprus. (5) And when they were at Salamis, they preached the word of God in the synagogues of the Jews: and they had also John to their minister. (6) And when they had gone through the isle unto Paphos, they found a certain sorcerer," now watch this; see, they're always bumpin' into these sorcerers. You say, "Well, we don't bump into 'em." What do they call politicians?—they're called religious leaders. Don't you get what a sorcerer is? It's somebody who works with a power other than God. If a person lives in deceptions and lies, they're a sorcerer-in-training. What does a sorcerer do? Deception! Deception! (6) "...they found a certain sorcerer, a false prophet,".... Oh wait a minute! He's religious too! "...a Jew".... No, he's a one-God person too! He goes to the temple and the synagogue. He comes to church and says, "Praise the Lord." "...whose name was Barjesus: (7) Which was with the deputy of the country, Sergius Paulus, a prudent man; who called for Barnabas and Saul, and desired to hear the word of God." I've often wondered how that could be. How could a man be a prudent, wise man, honorable, with integrity—runnin' with witches and runnin' with sorcerers? Why? Because the human spirit is so easily deceived.

I've asked you to pray two things tonight. I'm finishing in two minutes. Pray a third thing; one: Acts 4:29 (paraphrased) "Now Lord, grant thy servants boldness, that we make speak thy word by stretching forth thy hand, that signs and wonders and miracles be done by the name of thy holy child Jesus." Remember that? You need to pray for that. Second prayer: Lord, (Mark 16:20) "Help us as we go everywhere to try to be a light for you. Please grant us the confirmation of your word. Let the signs and the wonders confirm the word. We'll not take any credit, we'll not give out autographs, we'll not pose to get our picture taken. We'll tell everybody. If you confirm your word, it'll validate what we said." Acts 13:7 "Which was with the deputy of the country, Sergius Paulus, a prudent man, who called for Barnabas and Saul, and desired to hear the word of God." Last prayer request; I'm asking this church to pray everyday of your life, "God, please deliver me everyday from the spirit of deception."

Everyday of my life I pray that God would protect me from deception. I ask Him to protect me from seduction. I ask Him to protect to me from any kind of sexual misconduct. I ask Him everyday to protect me from a lust, or a greed for money, or power, or accolade, or position. I ask God to protect me from that stuff, but deception is the scariest thing in my life. You know why? A person who is immoral knows they're immoral, and a person who lies, cheats, and is dishonest, knows there are all of those things. When a person is deceived, they don't know they're deceived, because the deception of deception *is* deception. As the scripture says, that in the last days wonder working spirits will be unleashed on this planet, deceiving, devils that deceive, doctrines of devils that deceive. If you ever were gonna fall in love with the truth, you need to ask God to give you a love for the truth. I don't mean Acts 2:38 and beat everybody in the head with it. I'm talkin' about a love for the whole truth, for the Truth, for Jesus who is the Truth, for His Word that is the Truth, for the Holy Spirit of truth, for the body of Christ that ought to be an embodiment of the truth, principles of truth. With all the vile trash that's going on on this planet, God help us to be people of truth.

(Acts 13:8) "But Elymas the sorcerer (for so is his name by interpretation) withstood them, seeking to turn away the deputy from the faith." Now watch what I'm trying to tell you. Power Encounter: Light, Truth, Life, Holy Ghost, has its representative—Paul. Evil, error, wickedness, darkness, seduction, deception, has its representative—Elymas. "...And in this corner, weighing 225, 6'1, 52 knock-outs. And in this corner, wearing white trunks, comes in both doors...." You gotta get this: Acts 13; coming out of two corners—power encounter. One man standing up, full of the Holy Ghost; and another man standing up, full of the devil. The prize is the sheriff. Two kingdoms wanting one man, two representatives, two power sources, one is going away with the trophy. So Elymas, because this man desires to hear the word of God, he's hungry to know truth, Elymas tries to circumvent it and stop him from being saved.

Watch Paul (9) "Then Saul, (who also is called Paul,) filled with the Holy Ghost, set his eyes on him,..." he didn't say, "Oh, well, I'm sorry, I don't want to offend you...you wanna be a Baptist? Well... (10) "and said, O full of all subtlety and all mischief," yeah, he turned and said, "oh fool of all subtlety and mischief, you wicked, little, rotten bum, you, you evil adversary of death.... (10) "...thou child of the devil," how to win friends and influence people. No, no, no. There comes a time to be nice, and there comes a time to be just absolutely, down-right rough.

This man's soul was in the balance. He didn't know who was telling the truth. One had words, but now there's gonna be a power encounter; (10) "...thou enemy of all righteousness, wilt thou not cease to pervert the right ways of the Lord? (11) And now, behold, the hand of the Lord is upon thee," now it's no more games with words. We'll see who God is...God, I claim this soul for Calvary and for the power of Pentecost, and for the name of Jesus, You died for this man, this is a devil-possessed man, a liar, a deceiver; now let Your hand of chastisement and judgment fall on this man for two reasons: to stop the power of Hell, and to open up this man's understanding that he may realize that Jesus is alive, Jesus is the power of the universe, and Jesus is greater than anything he's having to deal with....

(11) "...and thou shalt be blind, not seeing the sun for a season. And immediately there fell on him a mist and a darkness;" now God didn't kill him, God just chastised him. God just let a quickening judgment fall on him. Bible said that he wouldn't see the sun for a season. God didn't kill him. Why? He wants him saved. He just said, "I'm not playin' games with this." Blind! That's easy. He did the same thing in Genesis 19 when those homosexual fags and queers tried to rape those angels. Bible says the angel just put his hand out and went, *phew*, struck them with blindness. Oh yes, oh yes! When they came down in 2 Kings 6 and Elijah's at Dothan and they came down to invade the place, God said, "Strike." The prophet said, "Strike them with blindness," and God said, "Sure," and the whole army is blind.

But here we are, we're just trying to give our tracts and CDs, we don't wanna offend anybody. Power encounter, scary stuff to be a real Christian. (11) "...and he went about seeking some to lead him by the hand. (12) Then the deputy, when he saw what was done, believed, being astonished at the doctrine of the Lord." Now that's the most monumental thing and I don't have to teach on it. Being astonished at the doctrine of the Lord.... What was the doctrine of the Lord? Here's what it was: Jesus is alive, Jesus is King of Kings and Lord of Lords, and Jesus is interested in the affairs of mankind, and the doctrine of the Lord is; if you get in the way of a soul being saved, God takes it personal. Astonished at the word of the Lord and "doctrine of the Lord."

I'm praying that God would somehow catapult us and move us into a level and a dimension that we would actually start believing that He want to use us daily in our lives, in power encounters. That when we meet people who are suffering and hurting, that we could give a word, that we could lay a hand on, we could have prayer, that we could confront evil, that we could find someone who's hurting, who's sick, and that somehow we would extend our hands as ambassadors of Jesus Christ. The great apostle Paul told us that we pray in Christ's stead—in the literal place of Christ. Lord, you gave Israel two gifts: You gave them Moses, who was the prophet, and you gave them Aaron, who was the spokesman for the prophet. You talked to Moses, Moses appointed Aaron, and Aaron did the miracles. Moses said that in the last days, God would raise up a prophet like unto Himself, that's you Lord. So You're the prophet and we now become Your Aaron and we become the demonstrators of the voice, the will, and the pleasure of the prophet Jesus. Lord, let the light shine on us and help us, I pray.

CHAPTER FIVE
Jesus was a man approved of God

The scripture says Jesus was a man approved of God by miracles and wonders and signs, which God did by Him. I believe, last week, I talked to you about the power encounter of the sorcerer, Elymas. Remember that? Acts 13, the power encounter between God's kingdom and Satan's kingdom. Satan's representative—the sorcerer. God's representative—Apostle Paul. There was a clash. One kingdom crumbled, the other one went on. That is supposed to be happening with us today. You will never win anybody to God with an argument. You have to have a demonstration. The world has to see that you've got something from another world if they're going to believe what you're saying. If not, then you're just another bunch of funny lookin' people who dress funny and act funny and talk funny. There's got to be a confrontation. There has to be a clash. Surely as the armies of the world train their trainees and their buck privates to be equipped to go out into warfare, so the Lord Jesus did for three and a half years—trained his disciples.

Now I really wish we could have some videotapes here...to have just spent two or three days with Jesus...and watched it all. If we could have watched Jesus, how he dealt with leprosy, every kind of disease, every kind of devil, how he dealt with hunger, how he dealt with sorrow, pain, funerals. I preach funerals—Jesus never did preach one. He stopped them all! He was just moved with compassion on the widow from the city called Nain, Jairus's daughter, and Lazarus. I told you before, it's worth repeating: Everybody that Jesus raised from the dead...those three instances...were all young people. Jairus's daughter was 12 years old, Lazarus was a young man and the widow's son was a young man. He didn't raise anybody that was old. Now, I don't think he had anything against old people. I just think in the mindset of God, He wanted the young people to fulfill their days and to walk in the things of God. I just wish that I could have seen how He dealt with it.

I am firmly convinced that the reason why Pentecostals have the greatest singers, musicians, praisers, worshipers and preachers, is because in every one of those areas we have been given mentors—examples on how to do it. We've sat under good teaching and preaching, and you assimilate not only the knowledge, but the wherewithal—how to function—protocol—what to do. You have good singers, good choirs and good musicians, not only because of what they do, but because of their example. That's why it's important that you sit next to someone who's a good praiser. Why? It's not just their noise; you learn. You learn what to pray by being with people who know how to pray. Your faith is mobilized when you hear from and hang around faith people. You just sit around someone who talks about the World Series all the time, talks about Baghdad, Afghanistan, the world economy, Hollywood, the world's going to Hell in a hand basket...and all that stuff is true, but it doesn't build your faith. It doesn't give you any courage or confidence to stretch. But you start hangin' around people who talk faith, miracles, possibilities, it-can-happen...it has a way of impacting you. I am firmly convinced that the reason why we are not more into miracles, signs and wonders...oh, we believe it...it happens among us...sporadically...once every 30 or 40 years, whether we need somebody healed or not.... The reason why is that we have no mentors. We have nobody to take us by the hand and say, "Here's how you do it."

Jesus was the master communicator, but He communicated not just principles, He communicated life-practices. He took His crew with Him and said, "Peter, James, John, you come with me. We're going to Jairus's house. Here's how you raise the dead." Now you may think I'm crazy, but if you read Mark 5, how Jesus raised Jairus's daughter from the dead...does anybody know what He did? First, He said, "The damsel's not dead, she's sleepin'." Secondly, He had to deal with all the critics and the unbelievers. What did He do with them? He put 'em out. Correct? Then He went inside, grabbed the damsel by the hand...watch...He did not pray for her, He spoke to her, "Little lamb, I say unto thee, arise," took her by the hand. She woke up. Now watch. Three guys are there; Peter, James, and John. Their jaws hit their sandals. "What manner of man is this, that death bows his knee to him?" "We saw him when he sent the sea to sleep." "We watched him when he dealt with devils and demons. Look at this!" I am firmly convinced that when Jesus walked out of Jairus's house that if He didn't wink—He smiled.

I am going to the New Testament. Go a few chapters in the book of Acts, and they hear that Simon Peter is in the area by Joppa. Dorcas has died. She was a wonderful woman. So they send for Peter that he might come. Wait a minute...what's he gonna do? The lady is dead as a hammer. Why are they sending for Peter?

"Well, Peter's been with Jesus."

"So?"

"Yeah, but he's learned some steps."

Now watch; he comes in...I guess I better turn to my Bible, you're lookin' at me like a communist or somethin'. My goodness, the chick got raised right off the paper.... Acts 9:32-34, "And it came to pass, as Peter passed throughout all quarters, he came down also to the saints which dwelt at Lydda. (33) And there he found a certain man named Aeneas, which had kept his bed eight years, and was sick of the palsy. (34) And Peter said unto him, Aeneas, Jesus Christ maketh thee whole: arise, and make thy bed. And he arose immediately."

Now where did Peter get that from? He was with Jesus at the pool of Bethesda in John 5 when Jesus said, "Arise, take up your bed and get outta here." They were with Him in Mark 2, when they let the man down through the roof and He forgave his sins. They were all gripin' and complainin', 'cause only God could do it and they're standing there with Jesus. That's the boss, they're just the followers. And He said, "That you might know that I have power to forgive sins also," watch, "young man, I say unto you, arise, take up your bed, go to your house." And he goes. Now watch: The master is gone and they are stuck with a situation, so what does Peter do? "I remember the boss. I remember how He did this." Aeneas, the Lord Jesus Christ makes you whole, arise, take up your bed and go."

You're not hearing me. The issue is; we need mentors and we don't have any floating around the United Pentecostal Church except T.W. Barnes, and he's busy. Guess what we're gonna have to do? Raise up our own, so that we can teach the next generation, "This is how it's done."

Remember the first time you ever watched somebody pray for the baptism of the Holy Ghost? Watched people gather 'round and make a bunch of noise, spit all over 'em, shake 'em, pray for 'em, and they got the Holy Ghost. Guess what? The next time you were at a rally or a church service...you did it! You didn't even know if it was really right or wrong, but..."that's what they did last time." What did you do? You learned by example!

Watch this: I am talking about Jairus's daughter...stay with me. Acts 9:36, Peter is at Joppa. "...a certain disciple named Tabitha, which by interpretation is called Dorcas: this woman was full of good works and almsdeeds which she did. (37) And it came to pass in those days, that she was sick, and died: whom when they had washed, they laid her in an upper chamber. (38) And forasmuch as Lydda was nigh to Joppa, and the disciples had heard that Peter was there, they sent unto him two men, desiring him that he would not delay to come to them. (39) Then Peter arose and went with them."

Now...Mark 5:22, they heard Jesus was in the area and Jairus runs to him, falls at his feet and says, "My little daughter lieth at the point of death: I pray thee, come and lay thy hands on her,..." watch; you always declare at the end what it is you want, "...that she may be healed; and she shall live." See, we have a problem with that. We're afraid to declare victory and healing until we see it feel it. Jairus said, "Come and lay your hand on her, she'll be healed." Most of us would say, "I hope she gets healed." Well, life and death are in the power of the tongue. You get what you say.... "Well, I hope she gets better." If they would've said that to Jesus, Jesus would've said, "Well, go home, we'll both hope together." But Jairus said, "You come lay your hand on her and she shall be well and be made whole." Jesus said, "Glad to do it. If that's what you believe, glad to do it."

But it got worse before it got better. Before He got there, the woman with the issue of blood detained him. She got healed, but Jairus's daughter had died, and someone from his house came and said to Jairus, "Don't trouble the Master, the child is already dead." Before Jairus can ever spit out any unbelief, Jesus turns and says, "Only believe and she shall be made whole." Now He's saying this after it's gone to the ultimate stage—death. Jairus showed his confidence in Jesus by not saying anything. He let the last statement to God-incarnate speak for him, "You lay your hand on her and she shall be made whole." He walks into the house...you know the story...all the people and professional funeral people were there, He throws them all out. Now watch this; watch the example here: Acts 9:39, "Then Peter arose and went with them. When he was come, they brought him into the upper chamber: and all the widows stood by him weeping, and showing the coats and garments which Dorcas made, while she was with them."

Guess what they're doing? They're showing no faith. They're saying, "It's over." They're doing what they did at Jairus's house; weeping and wailing and carrying on and saying, "It's over." Peter's got a spiritual flashback, déjà vu—"I was in something like this not too long ago. What was it that was like this? Stupid people crying and screaming and saying it's over. What happened here? Oh yeah! He threw 'em all out."

Next verse...he put 'em all out. Why? "Because if Jesus couldn't work with all that trash, I can't work, either." He's not trying to be unkind to people. He's trying to give us a picture that their doubt, their lack of faith, their unbelief, can hinder the best of us. He wasn't unkind to them. What was he doing? He was following the example of what Jesus had done at Jairus's house, so he put them all out. Those going out ain't resurrected nobody. The chick's dead. She's stiff as an ironing board. Right? Let me go a little further. There ain't anybody in this building that would want to be in his shoes. He was in that little room with the stiff and they're expecting somethin' to happen—not the people that were wailing, but the people who sent for him. Watch this...this is so powerful. Acts 9:40, "But Peter put them all forth, and kneeled down, and prayed..." That's the only thing he did that was different than Jesus. Jesus didn't have to pray. He was God-incarnate. He was in such union with the heavens, He said, "What I see the Father do, I do." "What I hear the Father say, I speak." "I do always those things that please my Father" so he could function. When He went to raise Lazarus, the only thing He did at Lazarus's tomb was that He did not pray to raise Lazarus.

According to John 11, when He started heading back to Bethany, they said;

"Where ya going?"

He said, "I'm going to see Lazarus." Watch. "I go to wake our friend."

"What do you mean, you 'go to wake him', he's dead as a hammer. He's been dead four days."

"I go to wake him."

Declared end results first. "I go to wake him." He didn't say, "I go to try." When He gets to the tomb, if you read the rest of John 11, He prays...not to wake him, He says, "I thank thee Father, that thou hast heard me. Thou always heareth me." Whoa, wait, when did He hear Him? Oh, way back a few days ago when He prayed. Once you've prayed, then it's time to act. And He comes, turns around, and says, "Lazarus, come forth." He says;

"Now I have said these things for those around me, that they might believe. I'm not praying to get power. I've got power. I'm not praying to get authority. I've got authority.

Lazarus, come forth."

You know why he said, "Lazarus, come forth"? Because He had already seen and heard in the Spirit Lazarus being raised. That's why He only healed one person at the pool of Bethesda. Just one! He didn't heal everybody. The Bible says there was a multitude of people at the pool, impotent, infirmed, diseased, problemed. He only healed one. Why didn't He heal the rest of them? Sovereignty of God. God, the Spirit, the living Spirit God, spoke to the humanity of the man, and said, "This man, today, at eleven o'clock." ...He walks right up to him and says, "Wilt thou be made whole?" Raised him up, he walked away and left the rest of them. There is your defense when your friends and fellow nincompoops tell you, "If you believe in healing and miracles and it's the will of God to heal sick, why don't you go to Shands and AGH and North Florida Hospital and empty 'em all?" Answer? Real easy. 'Cause Jesus didn't empty His Shands and North Florida Regional Hospital and AGH. You can only empty what God tells you to empty.

Let's try again. Acts 9: 40, "But Peter put them all forth, and kneeled down, and prayed..."
Don't know how long he prayed. This is what always gets me, "...and turning him to the body said..."

"Where'd you get that from, Pete?"

"That's what Jesus did in Jairus's house. He turned to the dead kid, grabbed her by the hand and said, 'I say unto thee, young damsel, arise'."

Peter turns around, turning himself to the body, says, "...Tabitha, arise. And she opened her eyes: and when she saw Peter she sat up. (41) And he gave her his hand..." boy, it's nervous in here right now. You're the people that damn and condemn everybody else that doesn't look and act and dress like you and doesn't believe like you. You're the people that do that. You're the people that say everybody's lost but you. Well, how come you don't believe this? You know why? Because you can be safe with doctrine and have no demonstration. Jesus said, "If you do not believe my words, believe the works that I do, that you might believe my words. For the works that I do testify to you that the Father has anointed me, approved of me and sent me." And even then, with all his works, tens of thousands of people, the Bible said multitudes, did not believe it and rejected him.

Peter said, "Tabitha arise, and she opened her eyes and when she saw Peter, she sat up. (41) And he gave her his hand, and lifted her up, and when he had called the saints and widows, presented her alive." Now here's what I want you to get, (42) "And it was known throughout all Joppa; and many believed in the Lord." In the previous example I read to you, Verse 35, "And all that dwelt at Lydda and Saron saw him..." Aeneas, the man that was healed...eight years crippled...and they all "turned to the Lord."

Do you know how long it would take for us to turn a city to the Lord with our fussin' and our cussin' and our standards and our dress and our doctrine and our arguments? But this guy got healed, and everybody knew he was sick and the whole city turned to the Lord! And when God used Peter to raise up Tabitha, all of Joppa turned to Lord! What am I saying? I'm saying that the supernatural demonstration of God is the most powerful evangelistic tool that God ever equipped His New Testament church with. It is! I've been talking about power encounters and all through Jesus' ministry it's one power encounter after another:

The naked streaker in Mark 5.

The Gadarene that had 2000 devils in him ran into Jesus, and when he did, the devils ran out of that man and went into the pigs—the pigs committed suicide.

Jesus met a man who was demonized, who the devil kept throwing in the fire and the water in Mark 9. Jesus confronts him, says, "Come out of him." Shakes him, makes him act like an epileptic seizure, throws him on the ground, Jesus picks him up.

It was always a power encounter. It was never, "You shouldn't do that, now let him go." No, it was force against a force. It was a kingdom against a kingdom. It was a King against another king. This scripture I read to you in Luke; He has this power encounter in the wilderness. He comes out in the power of the Spirit and then He goes into the synagogue and finds a guy in the synagogue that was full of the devil, and the guy turns around and says, "Let us alone." I say it over and over again; people who can tell the preacher, "Let us alone", you got a bad spirit, because only people with bad spirits tell preachers to shut up and let us alone.

So He cast the devil out of him and the people were astonished at His authority and His power, and so His fame spread. What happened? They began to bring people to Him by the thousands. There are two problems we gotta deal with: One is examples. If we don't have any mentors among us, then we have to take scriptural examples on how to try. Here's what we're afraid of: Suppose it don't work. Well, let me help you with it. You got your friends; they got leukemia, cancer, diabetes, heart trouble, pancreatic problems, whatever. Poor slobs are dying. They're slicin' and dicin' on 'em at the hospital day and night. Nobody damns and condemns those guys when the people die. They say;

"We did the best we could."

"Yeah, but she died!"

"Well, we did the best we could."

"But she died!"

Nobody ever says to them when their patients die, "You shouldn't have done that!" They did it because of compassion and learning and ability...to try and alleviate pain, sickness, and sorrow. That's what the medical field does, but we never demand the medical field to get it right. That's why they call it practice. "...We hope you survive the practice, and if you've got lots of insurance, we'll practice forever, we'll practice 'til we get it right, or you die." Now you're laughing, but that's the way the medical field works. Why? Because they don't claim to be God. They claim to be fine men and women who have educated themselves and are trying to alleviate pain and sorrow and sickness from people's bodies. And we give them tremendous fees. I mean hundreds of thousands of dollars. Six surgeries later, you ain't no better. You're like a stitched, raggedy doll. You got scars that have scars. And you walk out and they say, "Oh, well, we did the best we could." Nobody sues 'em! Nobody damns and condemns 'em, shoots 'em, burns down their home, murders their wife and children! They did what they could do. Isn't it funny that we will go to a doctor or surgeon or analyst and they are honest and sincere enough to say, "Well, this is a tough case here, we're gonna do what we can do. We're gonna try this and try that." And we say, "Try it." But now we get the spiritual, miracle stuff and we say, "We ain't gonna do none of that tryin'! You better do it right the first time, or I'll kill you." But you just paid this moron $146,000.00 to slice you from your ankle to your head and all he said was, "Well, we'll try this." And you don't ever get mad at them. They're your pals—Slice and Dice, and the Gang.

Interesting article in the paper this week...a hundred thousand plus people in the last two years, killed in America by misappropriation of medicine. A hundred thousand! You didn't burn the hospital down. We didn't shoot 'em. We just said, "Oh, well, they tried." Why are we afraid to try? If the Master said, "These signs shall follow them that believe; they'll lay hands on the sick and the sick will recover." If you can understand; you can't heal a headache anymore than you can give somebody the Holy Ghost, but you can pray in faith. Boy, it's quiet in here. Trying.... They call it in the medical field, "trial and error." Just keep trying. You get in the car repair field—and they just –"trial and error" 'til they make it work. But when we get into spiritual things, we don't think there's any room for trial and error. Really? You don't have any examples? The disciples tried to cast the devil out of that boy in Mark Chapter 9 and couldn't get it out. Jesus comes down off the mount of transfiguration, the Bible says that when Jesus talked to them, He didn't chew out the disciples for failing. He chewed the generation out, 'cause they didn't believe. Mark 9:19, "Oh faithless and perverse generation, how long shall I be with you?...bring him unto me." And when they start bringing the boy to Him, the devil tears him, throws him on the ground, makes Jesus look real bad. After he stops all that stuff He says to the devil; Alright, cut it out. Come out of him and don't ever enter into him again. Then the devil goes; Yes sir.

The disciples' jaws hit their sandals;

"Man, we've been workin' with this kid for six hours screamin' and yellin' and doin'...what's the deal? How come we couldn't get him out?"

"Well, this is a different kind of devil. You ain't met one like this before. This ain't a gutter demon that plays sex games and watches porno. No, no. This is a principality and a power. This is a demon that has authority over areas. He said, "You're not dealing with a buck private now, you are dealing with a lieutenant colonel. These boys require that your faith level be lifted and your faith level sometimes requires more prayer and more fasting."

So it wasn't that it wasn't the will of God to, and secondly, it wasn't that they didn't have authority and power. It's just that they had not stepped into that level. He shows 'em it was His will to make the boy well. He healed him in a second. Poof! What was that? Power Encounter.

"Well, Bro. Arnold, I just don't feel I have the power."

"When are you planning on gettin' it? You gotta ask God to help you. If you are not full of power and authority, you gotta ask God to help you. You can't keep going through your Pentecostal existence saying you're a Pentecostal and living like Church of Christ that doesn't believe in any miracles, and yet point to the menu and say, 'We believe this, we believe that, we believe this,' and the world is saying, 'You know, we've heard so much about the Word of God from you people, would there be any chance before we all die, could we see the God of the Word'?"

Stay with me.... When the Kingdom of God confronts the kingdom of evil, when Jesus meets Satan, there is a conflict and a clash. It will always be supernatural, and most of the time it will be messy. Consider the greatest power encounter recorded in human history is at a place called Calvary. It's creation shakin'. It's rocks splitting. It's the sun hiding its face in the atmosphere. It's the temple curtain being ripped in twain. It's graves from the earthquake shaking and throwing out dead carcasses on the ground. Now they didn't resurrect until Jesus was resurrected, but they did get exposed and get thrown on the ground, 'cause they couldn't get up 'til He got up, 'cause He's the first fruits. Consider what happened: two fronts clashing, two kingdoms clashing, two rulers clashing, hitting head-on; and from that power encounter, the human race is set free. Every sinner has hope of being forgiven. Every lost soul has a chance of coming to know God, because shaking on that tree, a naked, bloody man is bringing down a satanic kingdom.

It'll cost you something to do that, and that power encounter was followed by another power encounter. Ephesians 4 says that when they dropped that dead corpse in that tomb, the Spirit from that body came out of that body, and went to the pits of Hell itself. It says that He descended into the lower parts of the earth. He made havoc out of the underworld and the spirit world. He turned it upside down. He flipped tables left and right. He snatched the keys out of Hell's hand. He led captivity captive. He brought a resurrection of all the righteous dead out of the bowels of the earth, and the third day...here's another power encounter, because according the Acts 1, death tried to hold Jesus, and nothing was ever as strong in the world as death. It has held monarchs, tyrants, poor people, rich people, black folks, white folks, red folks, yellow folks. Nobody escapes from death, and death grabbed a hold of Jesus for a power encounter and Jesus just flexed His muscles and death went tumbling all over the place, and He came up out of the grave victorious over death, Hell, and the grave!

Then we have another power encounter. According to Ephesians 4; that when He rose from the dead, He ascended on high and led captivity captive. I don't know whether you understand what that means: When a Roman ruler, or a conqueror, conquered another nation, what they would do is openly demonstrate to their citizens that this guy had been beaten, and they dragged the conquered king behind the conqueror's chariot, so that everybody in their kingdom could see..."I whipped this guy, he's a prisoner, I got him chained to my chariot." You're not hearing me! When Jesus rose from the dead, He had chained behind his chariot: Satan, the imps of Hell, the powers of disease and death, every vile citizen of the kingdom, darkness, and wickedness. He led captivity captive and on the way up, He gave gifts to men. The Bible said in Colossians 2:11-14 that Jesus triumphed over Satan and the kingdom of evil, putting them to an open shame, publicly. What is He saying? He's telling everybody: "I beat him. I conquered him. I conquered him judicially. He's not in charge of you. I am deputizing you. I am making you my ambassador. You are going to be my body replacement. You are going to now become the second body of Christ. I was the first body of Christ, but I left this terra firma and ascended on high, but I have put my name on you and I have put my Spirit on you. I put my badge of authorization on you. Now, shame on you not doin' nothin'!"

According to Ephesians 4:8-10, Colossians 2:13-15, and Ephesians 1:17-23, Jesus is ascended on high. He's enthroned on the greatest throne in the universe. Watch. Principalities, powers, every name that is named in this world, and the one to come, have been put under His feet. Now we got a problem with that scripture. Here's why. Jesus is the head of the body. You are the feet. You know what the problem is? The one that you are stepping on to try to put under your feet, he's a rebel. He's a liar. He's an insurrectionist. He will not admit defeat even though he's lost his worldwide belt and he's lost his crown, and the whole spirit world knows that he's got his brains knocked out, and he's had his head crushed, but he's playing a game of deception with the church. He's saying, "Oh, I'm in charge. I got all the power I used to have. I got all the authority I used to have." Oh, no he doesn't! Oh, no he doesn't! You've got more power and you've got more authority and you've got more angels standing with you. Two out of three angels are standing with the church. You've got the Word of God, you've got the Spirit of God, you've got the blood of Jesus, you've got the promise of a destiny! That's why John can write, "Greater is He that is in you than he that is in the world!"

Anybody besides me ever hide money in your wallet? You ready for this? And then you forget you got it? I ran out of gas and walked almost 2 miles to go get a gas can. All the way back I had fifty dollars in my wallet. I stuck it away their probably five years ago. It's got mold on it. Couldn't pay for the gas, guy wouldn't even give me a lousy gas can; he wanted a five dollar deposit. I guess he thought I was an Islamic terrorist and I was going to steal it and blow up his gas station. Walked two and a half miles to my house to get my money, get back there, look in my wallet, I got $50 in there. Now you're looking at me and smiling saying, "Yeah." Now wait a minute. When you got the baptism of the Holy Ghost, God stuck stuff inside you, but sometimes we get intimidated by the situation. We get threatened by, "I'm gonna huff and puff and blow your house down." We get insulted by, "Well, who am I? I'm no great nobody." It has nothing to do with, "Who am I?" It has everything to do with "Who is He?" Peter wasn't the resurrection. Peter possessed the resurrection. I wonder how Peter felt that day, 'cause he hadn't ever raised anybody from the dead.

Because of Jesus' victory at Calvary and his victory at the resurrection...I am here in the fear of God to tell you that Calvary was never intended by God to be enough. Now I've heard preachers and I was a Southern Baptist and I was a follower of Billy Graham for many years. Calvary did...no it did not. Jesus, before He went to Calvary, said, "Except a corn of wheat fall into the ground and die, it abideth alone: but if it die, it bringeth forth much fruit." What was He saying? ...It is not enough for me to die and go down. I got to get back up.

Paul says if Jesus is not resurrected from the dead, Calvary's a sham, because the resurrection validates what Jesus did for you and I at Calvary. When He got back up, He had divine approval from Heaven. The Bible says He was raised by the glory of the Father. It's not over. When He ascends on high, according to Acts 2:33, when the Holy Ghost is poured out, that is a vindication and a validation of Jesus' ministry, because the Bible says that the Father in the heavens has accepted the sacrifice and has shed forth this which you now see and hear. So it takes Calvary, it takes the burial, it takes the resurrection, it takes the ascension on high, and it takes the descending of the Holy Ghost to put the package together.

Stay with me just a minute. Here's what I'm trying to tell you: Jesus' victory is forever and always irreversible. The problem is, we have been selected and chosen divinely by God to be living in the interim period, which is between the initial and the final culmination. Now the victory's already been won. The problem is; we're left here to enforce it. Though Satan has been defeated, he is still operating, he is still fighting, he is still deceiving. That's why the Bible says in Romans 7:21-23, "...when I would do good, evil is present with me." ...when I want to be nice, I'm not nice; when I wanna be powerful, I seem to be weak; when I want to be courageous, I seem to be just timid..... What's going on? ...There's a war in my members that are warring; when I would do good, evil is present.... The power of evil is still here. It's a defeated foe, but it ain't dead. Just like your Adamic nature is a defeated foe, but it ain't dead. You just stop praying a while and you watch ol' Adam get back on the throne.

Stay with me. So the church must enforce Jesus' legal victory in our daily lives, which requires the Holy Ghost, the power of God, faith in God. On June 6, 1944, the Allies invaded Normandy. Because of that victorious invasion, the defeat of the Third Reich and of Hitler's crazed people was inevitable. It was over. Once we invaded Normandy and started marching toward Berlin, the war was over. It wasn't until May 8, 1945, eleven months later and thousands of dead soldiers later that the final surrender was exercised. Why? Because the enemy fought to the death, retreating from Normandy all the way back to Berlin. They killed citizens, they murdered people, they blew up railroads, they tore up all kinds of food supplies. They blew up all kinds of water dams. They didn't want the allies to get anything. For though they were defeated and there was no way they could win, they kept fighting in retreat. You gotta hear me. Your adversary is in retreat. He's been whipped. He's been defeated but he's trying to intimidate you and say you ain't got power over him. He is a liar!

Well, if you don't believe my example, let me give you one from the six o'clock and the eleven o'clock news. The murdering rapist mongrel who lived in Baghdad, who raped women, and molested children, and murdered and tortured tens of thousands of people.... And we went over there and took his land. He's defeated. His whole thing is shot. Guess what? He's still fighting. But he's not sitting in the palace. He's underground with a handful of dirty renegades shooting one American today, two Americans tomorrow, killing six or seven innocent people here.... And we keep pressing the fight. And we keep pushing, until finally we can pull his head off his shoulders and flush him down the commode and get rid of him. Are you hearing me? His kingdom is in disarray, but he hasn't stopped fighting.

Osama Bin Ladin, that brave man who murdered all those people on September 11th...hiding in a cave somewhere. He's still fighting. He's still got his things going. He's not in charge. He's on the run. He's moving from one place to the next place to the next place. Your adversary is the same way. He's been defeated legally, judicially, and experimentally, but he still keeps fighting. Why? Because he knows that you don't believe who you are. Well.... We must see ourselves as God's spiritual soldiers, God's army involved in a real war. Therefore, we must be equipped with the power of the Holy Ghost allowing the Spirit of God to work in us and demonstrate, so that we can advance into the enemy's territory. And do what? Force the emancipation of souls of men and women, because that's the prize—men's and women's souls. The devil knows he's going to Hell, sentence has already been passed. He's got nothin' to lose to be vile and wicked and evil. He's trying to hold people's souls, and the only hope that they have is not a God in heaven; it's a church on earth.

You know the story of Ziklag? 1 Samuel 29 and 30. David was off somewhere and the enemy had come in and stole his wives and his children and stole all his cattle and his sheep and ran off with them. David is weeping and they're all...it's funny; those guys followed David until some problems. Reminds me of a church I pastor. ...follow the guy until some problems come up in their lives and then they beat up on the preacher. They were following David for years. "Man, David's our man. David's our boy." All the sudden, they had an invasion and they lost their children and their wives. They said, "Let's kill David." Not a one of those idiots said, "Let's pray." They all said, "Oh, no, this happened because of the guy leading us. Let's kill him." Now, I thought about that in my little, sick mind. And I thought; "Now wait a minute. You lost your wives, your children, your gold, your silver, your oxen, your sheep, your cattle. Now, what exactly do you get once you kill David? You still ain't got no wives and you ain't got no children and you ain't got no gold, and you ain't got no silver…oh and by the way, he's the only one God's talkin' to. He's the only one in the whole, dumb camp that ever could kill Goliath and you're gonna kill the only giant killer you got?"

So David, the Bible said, "encouraged himself in the Lord." You gotta learn to do that when you walk with God; "encourage yourself in the Lord." Guess what? Even in his disobedience, when he humbled himself before God, God answered him. And he said, "Shall I pursue?" And the Lord said, "Arise. Pursue. For thou shalt overtake them and recover all."

Don't you get it? Got wants the church to become so militant that we run into the enemy's camp and say, "I want my stuff back. I want my joy back. I want my faith back. I want my children back. I want my health back. I want my money back. I want the stuff given to me by a divine edict from God. I want my family saved. I want peace like a river. You came in and stole it from me, but God said I could come in and get it back!" Are you ready for this? Although it belonged to David and his crew, God would've let the Midianites and the Philistines keep it if they decided not to chase 'em. Watch. Stuff that we're supposed to have, we shoulda had it 50 years ago...God is standing back saying, "Go sit on your duff and just play church. Watch your little programs. Make believe you're in love with Jesus and I'll let your enemies keep all your stuff. But if you start seeking my face and start asking me, 'Can I get my stuff back', I'll give you some fresh direction. I'll give you some fresh courage. I'll give you a fresh anointing. And I'll let you go into the enemy's camp and I'll let you take back everything he stole!"

The problem is; the church, in general, is like America, in general. We no longer have a stomach to fight. All this crazy stuff that's on the news...all the Democrats damning and condemning Bush and all that stuff. You know where that's coming from? A people that have no stomach to fight. They thought that we could go into Baghdad, have nobody killed, take all their stuff, kill that bum, take everybody captive in 30 minutes...before the game was on. And now, all the sudden, it's gone months and months and months and billions and billions of dollars and people are dying here and dying there. We don't have no stomach. Now the thing is, "Let's pull out, let's come back and let him come back to power and rape all the women and kill all the children, 'cause we don't want any sacrifice." Anytime you get back what has been stolen from you, it's gonna cost you something. You're gonna have to be willing to get wounded, to get hurt, to get scratched in a tussle. The Bible said, "We wrestle not against flesh and blood", but we do wrestle. You know what we do? We want to shadow box. Why? "Well, first, no shadow's ever knocked me out. I've had a few hard fists knock me down, but I've never had a shadow hurt me, and I ain't ever afraid when I'm shadow boxing." Why? Shadows don't hurt you. He didn't say, "We box against the adversary." He said, "We wrestle." That means hands-on combat, gruntin', spittin'...aaaaahhhh...twistin', turnin', sweat, stink....aaaaahhhh.... And we say, "Why do we want to do that? Let's just go build us a church, have 'em sing, have 'em preach, let's go home." Well, what about the slaves that are captive? "Oh, forget them slobs, that's their own problem." Really? But that's what we were left here to do! He left us in charge to loose the captives.

At Pentecost, we had another power encounter. God gave birth at Pentecost to a warrior nation, an army of apostolic warriors. It was the reversal, at Pentecost, of Genesis 11 and the Tower of Babel when God came down and confused their languages, so they couldn't function. He reversed it at Pentecost, came down, did not confuse their languages, gave them languages to speak into the languages of all the civilizations that were at Pentecost in Jerusalem that day. For they spoke unto them of the wonderful works of God. And it indicted them and convicted them. When God came down at Pentecost, He did something that we desperately need in this assembly. He unified them. He took a bunch of separate people and made them amalgamated into one body, so that when Peter stands up at Pentecost to preach and the rest of the apostles stand with him, and the rest of the 120 stand there, everybody's behind him saying, "Amen." That's what brought such great conviction on those people. What would have happened if Peter stood up after he finished talking in tongues, and said, "These men are not drunk as you suppose, but this is but the third hour of the day and this is that which was prophesied by the prophet Joel" and about that time, some of the disciples had said, "Now, well, I don't know if that's really what that's about, you really think this is prophetic, Pete? Well, I think Pete's just too emotional, he's gotten carried away." You realize what a mess would have happened to everybody at the day of Pentecost if the people standing with Simon Peter were not standing with

Simon Peter?

Maybe you'll relate to this: You know what happens around here when I stand alone? When I preach 'til my tongue falls out and you're hoping we won't be late for lunch? I didn't say you did it...I'm using it as an example. If you read the book of Acts, here's what you have.... This will wake you up for a minute. Here's what you have: 28 chapters of the war chronicles of the first church. That's what that is. Twenty-eight chapters of a church at war with the kingdom of darkness. A church at war with a kingdom called Rome. A church at war with a kingdom called disease and devils and sickness and sin and lost people. It's the war chronicles! Man, you want to get your blood to jumpin', read Acts! It's the story of the first church; that they came with an invasion from Heaven and they took that invasion and they invaded their world.

The power principle presented in Acts 2 was this: the people are one. God unified the people. The people are one. Unity is the critical ingredient for power. They were together in one place. They were devoted to the apostle's doctrine. They had fellowship in Verse 42. Miracles, wonders, and signs occurred in Verse 43. They had one heart, one mind, and the apostles were used to give great power witness of what Jesus was.

And so I come to the conclusion of my Bible study. You've heard of Bro. Teklamariam in Ethiopia? Hard to believe a country like that has got almost 5 million Apostolics. Bro. Teklamariam said...because I was just with Bro. Seagraves in California, and he told Bro. Seagraves...because he asked him, "How do you get these crusades? How do you get these people saved in your country? How do you do it?" And Teklamariam, who's a very humble and sweet man, he said, "First place, we have a communist-ruled country. We are not free to do like you in America. We are not permitted to evangelize, nor cross-culture anybody." Watch this. He said, "Ninety-eight percent of the people that attend our big crusades (like Bro. Klinedinst had) came, because they were healed before. They experienced a miracle of deliverance before they ever heard our doctrine. And it was because God healed their children, raised their dead, did mighty things in their homes, that when we put a crusade on, these people come." Now he told us something else and I think it's mind-boggling. I hope I'm not boring you. He told us something else that's mind-boggling. He said, "We're not allowed to invite people to our churches, because of the government that rules Ethiopia."

So Bro. Seagraves asked him, he said, "Well then, how can your church run five million plus?"

He said, "Invariably, all the people that end up in our churches tell us angels tell 'em where to go."

He gave testimony after testimony of people coming to prayer meetings, cottage meetings, church meetings, knocking on the door.... He said that he asked this one lady, "How did you find us?" And she said, "The angel told me, 'take this bus to such-and-such a place, walk down such-and-such a street, go down so many doors, and you'll find the people that tell you the truth."

Now, right now, you're goin', "Oh brother...really?" Well let me help you with that. Example: Paul, Saul of Tarsus—knocked down blind. God wants to help him. He talks to Ananias and says; ...Go to a street called straight, to a such-and-such a place and you'll find a guy there who's blind, been prayin' and fastin' for three days.... Watch this; ...and he's seen a vision of you coming in and laying your hands on him and healing him....

No good, yet? Let me try it again: Cornelius, a devout man, centurion, loves God, fasts, prays.... Lost. Lost! Angel flies in the living room...I know why the angel came, because none of the Apostolics would. I'm not bein' unkind, I'm an apostolic. You know why they didn't go? There mind set was, "this was only for the Jews." See, it was their theology. Oh yes, it was their theology that was stopping them. They didn't think Jews were allowed to go to the Gentiles, so God gives him an angel and says; ...Look, you'll have to send for Simon Peter, because he won't come. Now he's got what it'll take to save you, but he won't tell you. It's not that he wants you to go to Hell; it's just that he's raised on the theology that says he can't go down to a Gentile.... That is a perplexing statement, because he has sent to find Simon Peter; watch this; who is already violating Hebrew theology, because he's with Simon the tanner and Jews were not allowed to hang around with tanners, 'cause they dealt with dead animals. So we only violate our theology when it's comfortable?

Cornelius has an angel. Simon Peter has a vision. God's gotta argue with him three times to get the guy with the truth to go. The angel only had to tell Cornelius once. See, the more truth we have, the less we want to spread past our comfort zone. It doesn't make us wicked people, it just makes us people. It's almost like you get into a routine of your life: you want your coffee this way, your tea this way, you eat your eggs this way, your pancakes that way, your toast is that way.... That doesn't make you a devil; it just makes you a people. You don't go to a restaurant and say, "Would you please fix me some eggs like I don't like em' and I'd like to have my coffee lukewarm, I love to have cream in my coffee, but don't give me any." You keep furniture in your house in the same place.... Don't matter whether it looks lousy, "I like it there, it stays there." Get you aggravated...you come home at night and your wife goes...I got a wonderful wife, I really do, but she has had times when she's gone into my garage and cleaned it up for me. She's kinda like a...she's kinda meticulous, clean kinda lady. Me? Everything is just piled, but I know where to find everything. I can lay my hand right on that screwdriver underneath a hundred pounds of wrenches. I know where my ruler is, I know where my pencil is. God love her, she goes out there and just puts everything in bins, I mean it just...and I'm goin', "...Where's my drill? Where's the chuck for the drill. Where's that...." Now, I oughta do it like her, 'cause once I learned it, it'd be real easy. You're not hearin' me.

I came home one time from a trip and she was aggravated, because I'm always getting annoyed about the closet. So she went and gets me a rack to put to my trousers on, and my shirts go here, my trousers go there...I can't find nothin'. I know where my brown suit is, where my beige pants are; they're right here. What..."Is there somebody else living in this house besides...my pants have been hangin' there for four years." Well, there over here on a rack....

The problem with power encounters; they're difficult to predict or control. They don't fit into our modern rationale and yet, all through Bible history, there's been power encounters.

I'm finishing right now. May 24, 1738, John Wesley's journal, watch this: "We had been praying with 60 of the precious brethren..." so his diary says. Watch this: "...and about three A.M. in the morning..." that would kill all of this church, "...three A.M. in the morning the power of God fell on us. Men and women fell down. Many lay prostrate, intoxicated, speaking in heavenly languages...."

Watch this: "As soon as some were able to recover from the presence of His majesty, we began to extol Him with one voice. 'We praise Thee Oh Lord God of Heaven and acknowledge Thee to be the Lord'." That is not permitted in the modern Methodist assembly today. Our idea of church order does not always match God's. Sometimes I think we don't really need to cast away our order, that's crazy; we just need to ask God to readjust our order, so it meets His order.

(Closing prayer)
Jesus, I thank you so much. I thank you for all the people that have listened to me and I hope and pray that somehow, everybody has some way been impregnated with the principles of the truth that I tried to share; that we must stir ourselves and shake ourselves and go after the holy things of God, for I know that You will let us live without the Holy Ghost if we don't want it, and You will let us live with the Holy Ghost, but never be a threat to Hell and never be a rescue mission for the souls of mankind. I ask You to help us. I ask You to send a stirring into our hearts. I pray that we become God hungry, desperate for a power encounter with God, so that we can fulfill the mission that You've left us to do: to save the lost, to enforce the benefits and the blessing of Calvary and Pentecost. Please deliver us from apathy and lethargy, and I-don't-care-itis. Please help us. Please talk to us and deal with us, challenge our spirits and our hearts. Somehow, help us to improve our personal prayer lives. Give us a fresh hunger and thirsting for Your presence, for the power of God to work. God, give us some people that will pray everyday that the gifts of the spirit would begin to operate among us more fruitfully and more frequently, that the glory of God would be made manifest in our lives. In Jesus' name I pray.

ORDER INFORMATION

Please call us, or see our web site at www.gainesvilleupc.net for the most current listing of all books in print by Rev. Jeff Arnold, including:

"The Why & Wonder Of Worship Book One- Volumes One, Two & Three"
"The Why & Wonder Of Worship Book Two- The Final Series"
(Transcribed as Rev. Arnold taught on the subject of Worship)

"Five More Minutes"
(many years of inspiring Sunday Bulletin articles)

"The Pulpit Of Pastor Jeff Arnold"
In text, a Computer CD-Rom in PDF format containing
"The Why & Wonder Of Worship Book One"
"Five More Minutes"

"Pulpit Notes"
a continuing series of volumes
(a written record, ideal for study, of the high points in the teachings of Rev. Arnold from selected subjects)

CHECK WITH US PERIODICALLY FOR NEW TITLES

THE PENTECOSTALS OF GAINESVILLE
TRUTH PUBLICATIONS
8105 NW 23rd Avenue
Gainesville, FL 32606
PHONE: (352) 376-6320 FAX: (352) 376-7105
www.gainesvilleupc.net